TRANSMIGRATION IN INDONESIA

TRANSMIGRATION IN INDONESIA

J. M. HARDJONO

KUALA LUMPUR
OXFORD UNIVERSITY PRESS
JAKARTA LONDON MELBOURNE
1977

Oxford University Press
OXFORD LONDON GLASGOW NEW YORK
TORONTO MELBOURNE WELLINGTON CAPE TOWN
IBADAN NAIROBI DAR ES SALAAM LUSAKA ADDIS ABABA
KUALA LUMPUR SINGAPORE JAKARTA HONG KONG TOKYO
DELHI BOMBAY CALCUTTA MADRAS KARACHI

● *Oxford University Press 1977*

Printed in Singapore by Printers & Converters (Pte) Ltd.
Published by Oxford University Press, Lot 3, Jalan 13/3, Petaling Jaya, Selangor, Malaysia

For Dr. Claire de Ranitz,
who, in a life-time of service,
has done so much for the sick
and needy of Indonesia.

Foreword

In the second chapter of his great *History of Java* (1817) Stamford Raffles made a remarkable forecast. Having in 1815 estimated that that island supported a population of 4·6 million, he proceeded to argue that only about one-seventh of its cultivable land was yet utilized and, assuming that the population would double every hundred years, he concluded that Java could provide adequately for such growth for another three centuries, after which migration might take place into the relatively empty territories of Sumatra, Kalimantan and other neighbouring islands.

Although Raffles' figure of 4·6 million inhabitants in Java in 1815 has since been criticized as an underestimate, it is noteworthy that the first small-scale Dutch attempt at what rather curiously came to be called transmigration, or in other words the organized transfer of population from one island to another, was made from Java to Sumatra when the population of Java reached 30·4 million, which was very nearly seven times Raffles' estimate of 1815. Yet, so far from having taken three centuries to reach this total, the population of Java was recorded as 30·4 million in the census of 1905.

From that time forwards at least 63 per cent of Indonesia's total population has lived within Java and Madura, which together contain a mere 7 per cent of the country's territory. While in respect of soil, climate and relief, the greater part of Java is distinctly better suited for intensive rice cultivation than the other major Indonesian islands, this alone does not explain why its population density is more than twenty times that of the remaining 93 per cent of the country. Reduced to its simplest terms, the basic cause of this extraordinary discrepancy is that during the greater part of the colonial period the Dutch concentrated their attention overwhelmingly on this most favoured of all the islands and, in providing it with a highly efficient infrastructure and related facilities for their own purposes, they had already begun significantly to reduce the death rate well before the end of the nineteenth century.

Nevertheless, by the early decades of the present century the continuing growth of numbers in Java was clearly accompanied by declining nutritional standards, and when to these difficulties were added the unexpected problems caused by the great depression of the 1930s, the Dutch administration turned once again—but this time far more seriously—to transmigration as a means of staving off even greater distress in the congested countryside of Java. In the event, however, this amounted to only a marginal palliative, and it was not until much more recent times that independent Indonesia has found out for itself that the way forward is not to export the rural poverty of Java by transmigrating peasant families to similarly small plots, usually of poorer soil, in other islands, but instead to draw upon the surplus labour of Java to carry out pioneer developmental tasks of many kinds in these outer islands whose natural potential cannot yet be effectively exploited by the limited resources of local manpower.

The exciting prospects which this new approach makes possible are now beginning to capture the imagination of a new generation of forward-looking young Indonesians, and in this context Mrs. Hardjono's book represents an exceptionally timely contribution to the geographical literature relating to this great country.

University of London,   CHARLES A. FISHER
September 1975

Acknowledgements

I wish to express my gratitude to Maj.-Gen. R. Soebiantoro, Director-General of Transmigration, for his interest and assistance during the writing of this book. My thanks are also due to officials of the Directorate-General for Transmigration and the provincial-level Transmigration Directorates for the many useful conversations I had with them and for the information they provided. I wish to emphasize, however, that all opinions and interpretations expressed in the book are mine and for them I take all responsibility.

Finally, my thanks to Professor C. Fisher, who read the manuscript and made several helpful suggestions about its contents.

Bandung,   J. M. HARDJONO
Indonesia,
June 1975

Contents

Tables

Maps

Introduction

INDONESIA, like many other countries in the world today, is feeling the effects of over-population. As population increases, unemployment also increases and per capita income falls. Indonesia, however, unlike many other densely populated countries, has the advantage of unused land. In past years, migration programmes have been undertaken in an attempt to shift some of the underemployed population of Java, Madura, Bali and Lombok to other parts of the Indonesian archipelago.[1] Yet results so far have not been very satisfactory and today, three-quarters of the way through the twentieth century, overpopulation is causing Indonesia to remain one of the poorer nations of the world, in terms of per capita income, despite comparatively abundant natural resources.

Indonesia is usually classed as one of the 'developing' countries. The outsider tends to think of the country as a group of islands on the fringe of the South-East Asian mainland and to overlook the fact that this nation ranks fifth in the world in terms of the size of its population. The census taken in 1971 revealed that in that year the population was just over 119 million, which places Indonesia immediately behind China, India, Russia and the United States of America. Indonesia's population today is far in excess of that of neighbouring South-East Asian countries like Malaysia, the Philippines and Thailand, which together have less than 100 million people.

Added to this is the relatively high rate of population growth. In 1971 it was found that the population was increasing at a rate of 2·37 per cent annually. Although some parts of South-East Asia have higher rates, the Indonesian rate of growth is certainly not a low one, for it means an annual increase in population of more than 2½ million people. Assuming that the same rate of growth continues, the population will be at least 200 million by the end of the century.

Indonesia has extensive natural resources that could, if utilized efficiently, support the present population at a much higher standard of living. Apart from large reserves of petroleum, the country has other mineral deposits, including copper, bauxite, tin and nickel, some of which have as yet been barely touched. In addition, there are forest lands not yet fully exploited. But today population problems are becoming more and more evident in certain parts of the country.

As has been found in other developing countries, it is not easy to slow down population expansion, even when finances are made available for family planning campaigns. Where educational levels are still relatively low, people cannot be readily convinced that they must limit the size of their families in their own and the nation's interests. Now in the 1970s a great deal of attention is being given in Indonesia to the task of spreading a knowledge of contraception, with financial and other support from various international organizations. The present campaign is certainly rather belated in its appearance; such steps should have been commenced many years ago. It will be another generation before the real impact of the present campaign is felt, and even then the rate of population growth will decrease only slowly.

In fact, Indonesia's present demographic problems tend to centre around the maldistribution of population rather than around the actual size of the population, and thus the problem is somewhat different from that now being faced in India, for example. A mere glance at figures for the population of each major island in the archipelago reveals this. Java and Madura, with 6·64 per cent of the land area of Indonesia, had 63·83 per cent of the country's population in 1971; the four larger islands—Sumatra, Kalimantan, Sulawesi and Irian Jaya[2]—were relatively underpopulated, with only 29·7 per cent of the total population.

A significant factor in all population considerations is the very low geographic mobility of the Indonesian population, which means that labour is relatively limited in movement. Thus, although in many parts of Java overpopulation has resulted in unemployment or underemployment, lack of labour presents a problem in other islands. Internal migration within the country is not extensive, and although every year a certain number of people move from Java to settle elsewhere in the archipelago, a comparatively large number also move into Java. It is difficult to give exact figures for the number who move permanently into Java, but it is significant in view of current population pressures.

It would appear then that many of Indonesia's present problems in the economic sphere could be solved with a more even distribution of population. But to say, as people often casually do, that the government should 'shift some of the people' is to ignore the reasons for this maldistribution of population and the difficulties inherent in any attempt to move large numbers of people from one island to another, even within the same country.

The problem of overpopulation is made more acute by the structure of the economy, which is very much one-sided. Most of the people of Indonesia obtain their livelihood from agriculture. But farm incomes in Java and Bali are extremely low, since each plot of land has to support a large number of persons. Rural poverty is increasing as population grows, and all development undertakings are slowed down by this fact. The disparities that exist between city and village are becoming more striking, as are those between the more developed parts of urban Java and the other islands of the archipelago, where farm incomes are equally low not so much because of population pressure as because of existing forms of land utilization.

Today, regional development is seen as being essential for, if not synonymous with, national development. This implies development of the potential existing in one form or another in all of the provinces of Indonesia, both in Java and in the other islands. The emphasis at the present time is upon agricultural development, as a necessary preparation for industrial expansion in later years. In Java agricultural development involves intensification in existing farming areas, but outside Java it means an extension of the land under permanent cultivation. However, the lack of manpower forms a major obstacle to economic growth in the other islands of the archipelago. Agricultural expansion is hindered by the fact that these islands are sparsely populated. Expansion in mining and forestry is likewise handicapped by lack of labour for work directly and indirectly connected with such undertakings.

The term 'transmigration' is used in Indonesia to mean

... the removal and/or transfer of population from one area to settle in another area determined upon within the territory of the Republic of Indonesia, in the interests of the country's development, or for other reasons considered necessary by the Government.[3]

It thus covers government-organized schemes and those undertaken by non-government bodies for the resettlement of people, as well as migration by individuals or groups of individuals who move to project areas of their own accord and with only a small amount of assistance. The term is not intended to include completely independent migrants from Java and Bali who settle in other islands without the knowledge and sponsorship of the transmigration agency or those people who move to Java from the other islands of Indonesia.

The planned and guided migration of large numbers of people from Java, Madura, Bali and Lombok can make an important contribution to economic development in the other islands. Transmigration today is seen as a rural development programme in which the aim is to utilize the agricultural potential of less populous areas by providing the manpower needed for agricultural expansion. In that sense it is a land settlement programme, similar in some but not all respects to programmes carried out in recent years in other parts of South-East Asia. While the impact of such migration upon population densities in the areas from which migrants move will be negli-gible as long as birth rates remain high, the full significance will be seen in future years in the economic growth made possible in other parts of the country by an increase in popula-tion.

This book is an attempt to look at some of the reasons for the maldistribution of popula-tion in Indonesia, to examine the extent to which transmigration projects have been suc-cessful in the past and to consider the policies now being formulated for the transmigration programme in coming years.

[1] The word 'archipelago' is used throughout to mean the land within the territory of the Republic of In-donesia.

[2] The name of this province (formerly Irian Barat, that is, West Irian) was changed officially to Irian Jaya on 1 March 1973. Here and throughout the book the new Indonesian spelling, introduced on 17 August 1972, is used for place names and Indonesian words.

[3] Definition given in Clause 1 of the Basic Transmigra-tion Act of 1972.

1

The Indonesian Population Problem

Population Distribution

IN 1971, when the most recent census was taken, Indonesia had a population of 119 232 499 people; with an annual increase of over 2·5 million, the population in 1978, close to the end of the Second Five-Year Development Plan, will be approximately 141·6 million.[1] The census taken by the Dutch colonial government in 1930 had placed the total number of people in the country at 60 727 233; thus in a period of forty-one years, the population almost doubled. According to the 1971 census, the present rate of growth is 2·37 per cent per year, which means that the estimate (in which allowance has been made for the anticipated effects of the present family planning campaign) of a population of 200 million in the year 2000 is not unrealistic.[2] In fact it appears highly likely that the 200 million mark will be reached some years before the end of the century, as Widjojo Nitisastro's projections for the year 1991 suggest.[3]

Of the Indonesian population, a very large percentage is, and will continue to be, concentrated on the island of Java. Table 1 shows the distribution of population according to the major islands, as found in the 1930, 1961 and 1971 censuses. There seems little doubt that Java has always been the most populous island in the archipelago, as a consequence of its advantages as far as human settlement and agriculture are concerned. Within Java, however, there are concentrations of population not apparent from the figures given in Table 2 for population distribution by province. In

Table 1
Population of Indonesia by Area and Density, 1930, 1961 and 1971

Island(s)	1930		1961			1971		
	Population in thousands	Density per sq km	Population in thousands	Density per sq km	Area in sq km	Population in thousands	Density per sq km	Area in sq km
Java and Madura	41 718	316·1	62 993	477	132 174	76 102	565	134 703
Sumatra	8 255	17·5	15 739	33	473 606	20 813	38	541 174
Kalimantan	2 169	4·0	4 102	7·6	539 460	5 152	9	550 848
Sulawesi	4 232	22·4	7 079	37	189 035	8 535	37	227 654
Other islands	4 353	7·6	7 106	12·4	570 070	8 630	15	572 708
Total	60 727	31·9	97 019	51	1 904 345	119 232	59	2 027 087

Source: 1930 census figures from Widjojo Nitisastro, *Population Trends in Indonesia*, Cornell University Press (Ithaca, 1970), p. 75.
1961 census figures from *Sensus Penduduk 1961 Republik Indonesia*, Biro Pusat Statistik (Jakarta, 1962), p. 15.
1971 census figures from *Statistical Pocketbook of Indonesia, 1970 & 1971*, Biro Pusat Statistik (Jakarta, 1972), pp. 24-5.

Note: Areas of the major islands were the same in the 1930 and 1961 censuses; the figures used in the 1971 census are somewhat larger, particularly in the case of Sumatra and Sulawesi.

2

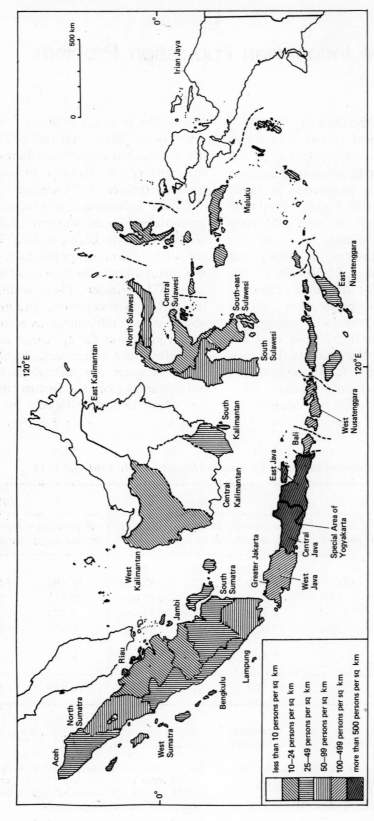

Map 1: Indonesia: population distribution by province (based on 1971 Census)

500 km

0°

120°E

Irian Jaya

Maluku

North Sulawesi

Central Sulawesi

South-east Sulawesi

South Sulawesi

East Nusatenggara

East Kalimantan

West Nusatenggara

120°E

South Kalimantan

Bali

Central Kalimantan

East Java

West Kalimantan

Greater Jakarta

Special Area of Yogyakarta

West Java

Central Java

Jambi

South Sumatra

Riau

Lampung

Bengkulu

West Sumatra

North Sumatra

Aceh

0°

less than 10 persons per sq km

10—24 persons per sq km

25—49 persons per sq km

50—99 persons per sq km

100—499 persons per sq km

more than 500 persons per sq km

Table 2
Population of Indonesia by Province and Density, 1971

Province	Population	% of total population	Area in sq km	% of total area	Density per sq km
1. Greater Jakarta	4 576 009	3·84	576	0·03	7 944
2. West Java	21 632 684	18·14	49 118	2·42	440
3. Central Java	21 877 081	18·35	34 503	1·70	634
4. Yogyakarta Area	2 489 998	2·09	3 140	0·15	793
5. East Java	25 526 714	21·41	47 366	2·34	539
6. Aceh	2 008 918	1·68	59 814	2·95	34
7. North Sumatra	6 622 693	5·55	70 804	3·50	94
8. West Sumatra	2 793 196	2·34	66 080	3·26	42
9. Riau	1 641 591	1·38	124 084	6·12	13
10. Jambi	1 006 084	0·84	62 150	3·06	16
11. South Sumatra	3 443 749	2·89	103 268	5·09	33
12. Bengkulu	519 366	0·44	21 082	1·04	25
13. Lampung	2 777 085	2·33	33 892	1·67	82
14. West Kalimantan	2 019 936	1·69	157 066	7·75	13
15. Central Kalimantan	699 589	0·59	156 552	7·72	4
16. South Kalimantan	1 699 105	1·42	34 611	1·71	49
17. East Kalimantan	733 536	0·62	202 619	9·99	4
18. North Sulawesi	1 718 155	1·44	24 289	1·20	71
19. Central Sulawesi	913 662	0·77	88 561	4·37	10
20. South Sulawesi	5 189 227	4·35	82 768	4·08	63
21. South-east Sulawesi	714 120	0·60	32 036	1·58	22
22. Bali	2 120 338	1·78	5 623	0·28	377
23. West Nusa-tenggara	2 202 333	1·85	21 740	1·07	101
24. East Nusa-tenggara	2 294 945	1·93	48 889	2·41	47
25. Maluku	1 088 945	0·91	83 675	4·13	13
26. Irian Jaya	923 440	0·77	412 781	20·36	2
Indonesia	119 232 499	100·00	2 027 087	100·00	59

Source: 1971 Population Census (Preliminary Figures) *Statistical Pocketbook of Indonesia 1970 & 1971,* Biro Pusat Statistik (Jakarta, 1972), p. 4 and pp. 24-5.

certain parts of the island, densities are already far greater than the average of 660 persons to the sq km predicted for Java and Madura in 1978 on a basis of the findings of the 1971 census.[4] The Shire of Klaten in Central Java had a density of 1 486 to the sq km in 1971, while the density in the Shire of Bantul in the Special Area of Yogyakarta was 1 375 to the sq km. Seven other shires (*kabupaten*) in Java already had densities of more than 1 000 persons to the sq km in the same year. Certain parts of Bali, notably the Shire of Gianyar, have for many years had densities well over the average figure of 377 to the sq km. A few densely populated areas are also to be found in the other islands of Indonesia, the most populous being around Medan in North Sumatra, Bukittinggi in West Sumatra, Metro and Pringsewu in Lampung, Ujung Pandang in South Sulawesi and the Hulu Sungai area in South Kalimantan.

One significant aspect of the Indonesian population structure, by no means uncommon in developing nations, is the high percentage of children under 14 years of age. The 1961 census revealed that 42·1 per cent of the total population was 14 years old or less, while the 1971 census found that almost exactly 44 per cent came into this age group. The implications for the labour force have been pointed out by Widjojo: '. . . during the ensuing decade (1966–76) the consequence of past events will be a radical rejuvenation of the working-age population in the form of an almost doubling of the number of younger workers aged 15-19 and 20-24 years'.[5] This is already apparent in the increased unemployment throughout Indonesia and particularly in Java.

Indonesia today, despite a relatively large land area, reasonably abundant natural resources and extensive supplies of labour, remains one of the less developed countries of the world. If per capita income is taken as a measure of economic prosperity, then Indonesia ranks far behind her neighbours. In 1972, the Indonesian per capita income was estimated at only US$97.[6] Although it is true that definite economic growth has been taking place in the years since 1968, the increase in the country's population more than balances any real progress in the economy. In other words, the 7 000 or so people born each day in Indonesia keep the per capita income low and will continue to do so. While per capita income should not be used as the only criterion for measuring economic development, it does reveal the problems of economic expansion in relation to population growth.

One consequence is that a relatively high percentage of national income has to be spent on the import of foodstuffs, textiles and other consumer goods. In 1973–4, of the US$2 978 million spent on imports, US$949 million were used for such goods; of this

amount, $438 million went to rice imports alone.[7] While it is true that a much smaller percentage today is used for imported foodstuffs and textiles than in the early 1960s, and a much higher precentage is spent on capital goods, nevertheless the cost of feeding and clothing Indonesia's population is still great. At the same time, exports of certain agricultural products have declined because of increased home consumption, though other factors are involved, such as a decrease in productivity per hectare and the conversion of land once used for the production of export crops to the cultivation of food crops.

Economic Problems in Rural Java

Despite the move to urban areas of relatively large numbers of village people, overall population growth is such that pressure on the land in areas of permanent cultivation is increasing steadily. The situation is obviously at its worst in Java. The 1963 Agricultural Census revealed that in both West and Central Java the average size of holdings was 0·69 hectares, while in East Java it was 0·76 hectares and in the Special Area of Yogyakarta 0·58 hectares.[8] In the Special Area of Yogyakarta, 59 per cent of holdings were less than half a hectare in size in 1963. The arable land used for agriculture in Java and Madura was 0·12 hectares per capita in 1964, by comparison with 0·155 hectares in 1955.[9] As might be expected, there is a high percentage of landless agricultural labourers in most rural areas. Although land reform measures have been introduced in Indonesia, their application has not altered the picture very much.[10] Even if implementation were carried out more strictly than has been customary, the situation would not change very greatly, since Java has never had the large holdings found in the past in other parts of South-East Asia.

The consequences of overpopulation are already becoming apparent in Java and Bali. For centuries the farmer has been obtaining high returns from the soil; even today, productivity is remarkably high in many districts of these islands, with very little or no use of fertilizers. But with the increasing demand for arable land and for food crops in areas like the Upper Solo River basin, farmers have cleared hillsides that are far too steep for any sort of rice cultivation.[11] In most cases cassava is planted, but after harvesting the soil is left without vegetative cover. The heavy, often torrential, rains of the wet season then carry off inches of top soil, leaving bare hills exposed to the erosive effects of wind and of further deluges of rain. At the same time soil fertility has decreased significantly because of continued planting of cassava. Such land is useless for farming, and, while reforestation schemes exist, little has been done to ensure that something is planted on such slopes. In fact, reforestation work is often hampered by village people who, ignorant of the real significance of replanting trees, continue to cut them down.

In many districts, the same process of deforestation has taken place not to obtain more farming land but to obtain a source of fuel. For the poorer classes, wood is the fuel commonly used for cooking purposes. Village people cut down trees for their own use and also, more frequently, for sale in nearby urban areas where lime kilns, tile and brick factories, small bakeries and households provide a ready market.[12] It is impossible to make an estimate of the numbers of people who earn their living or else supplement their farm incomes in the dry season by collecting and selling firewood. The noticeably bare slopes of much of Java today give some indication, however, of the extent to which it is happening.

In recent years Java has suffered from serious floods. While it is true that floods have always been a part of the natural cycle in Java, the fact remains that they are becoming more serious. To the farmer who knows little of what happens beyond his own immediate vicinity, the cause may appear to be unusually heavy rain. Yet even in years like 1972, when the rainfall has been below average, floods have occurred in many parts of Java. Deforestation in the uplands is the real reason why the lowland farmer is finding that the big rivers draining the plains overflow their banks more frequently than they did thirty years ago. The Brantas, Solo and Citarum, together with the smaller rivers of Java, carry down vast quantities of water that cannot flow out into the Java Sea quickly enough. Hence rapid siltation is occurring and the beds of rivers are raised considerably. The construction of levees cannot prevent the floods that occur annually on much of lowland Java. All these factors indicate that the balance which once existed in Java has been destroyed, and with increasing pressure on the land, the situation will certainly not improve.

Farm incomes are low not just because of population pressure, however. One basic problem is that the farmer receives a relatively small percentage of the final price of his products. The *ijon* system by which unripe crops are sold to a broker by farmers in need of money is part of the pattern of life in many areas of rural Java. The government is making every effort to overcome such problems by the establishment of village banks and Village Enterprise Units (*Badan Usaha Unit Desa*)[13] that can provide fertilizers and other inputs needed by the farmer at a reasonable price, market his produce directly and also provide credit when he needs it.

Population pressure means unemployment or at least underemployment. Many farmers, and even more so landless farm labourers, are occupied for only part of the year, during the wet season; where irrigation is not available, rural activities are very limited during the dry months. Further intensification, particularly in rice cultivation, by means of the *Bimas* programme, is making larger supplies of basic foodstuffs available each year. Indonesia was nearing the long-desired goal of self-sufficiency in rice production when the disastrously prolonged dry season of 1972 affected the expanding economy rather seriously.[14]

Agricultural intensification, however, though certainly necessary if productivity and farm incomes are to be raised, does not open up new employment opportunities, nor does it give farms to landless agricultural labourers. Labour-intensive projects, involving mainly construction of roads and irrigation canals, have been undertaken by the government, primarily in areas where food production is low, in an attempt to provide work, which is paid for with food and a small amount of money.[15] However, increasing population pressure will ultimately reduce the achievements of all these efforts in rural areas.

Meanwhile, the flow of people to the cities is continuing. According to the 1971 census, 17 per cent of Indonesia's population lives in rural areas (by comparison with the 1961 census figure of 15 per cent).[16] Urbanization has given rise to many problems, for the existing cities cannot handle the huge populations living in them—huge, that is, in relation to available facilities like housing, running water, electricity, paved streets, public transport, schools and hospitals. The population in the Capital Territory of Jakarta, for example, increased from 811 000 in 1930 to 2 907 000 in 1961 and to 4 576 000 in 1971. Even allowing for the high birth rate, it is obvious that a large number of people must have moved into the city area in this period. Other cities have the same problem of village people, as well as people from the smaller towns, drifting to urban areas in search of employment. All attempts to 'close' the larger cities to incoming people have proved unsuccessful because of the economic pressure of unemployment in rural areas.

Added to this pattern of village people moving to the cities of Java is the movement of people from Sumatra and the other islands into Java in the hope of attending better schools and universities, of earning a better livelihood and of enjoying a better standard of living. It is difficult to give precise figures for the number of people who settle permanently in Java but it may be noted that: 'the flow of people from other regions to Java and Madura has been estimated as two or three times greater than the results achieved by transmigration up to the seventies'.[17]

Industrialization is no final answer to the problem of unemployment, though an expansion in industry is certainly desirable in the one-sided Indonesian economy. Industries are increasing steadily, but they absorb only a relatively small number of extra workers, for industrialization tends to involve undertakings that are, for the most part, capital-intensive rather than labour-intensive. There is a growing realization in Indonesia today that the use of advanced technology in the expansion of existing industries and the establishment of new ones is not really advantageous. Yet although the government is conscious of the need to promote industries using intermediate technology and to encourage the modernization of home industries without reducing the numbers of workers employed, it has not proved easy to put these principles into practice. The textile industry is one example of how the advanced technology used in recently established mills is helping to push out small producers, who would be in a better position to compete if they had some of the advantages of intermediate technology.

Solutions to the Problem

Any attempt to find solutions to Indonesia's population problems must inevitably be focused upon control of population growth not just in Java but also in other parts of the archipelago where densities are increasing rapidly. In the years since 1968, serious attention has been given to a birth-control campaign, to which the present government is fully committed. The Second Five-Year Plan states that: 'family planning is the basic undertaking in population policies in general and in efforts to reduce the birth rate in particular'.[18] Neglected in past years more because of lack of awareness of the seriousness of the problem than because of religious objections, family planning is now being actively encouraged by the government, which, with the assistance of certain international organizations, has made funds available for the establishment of clinics, the training of field workers and population education programmes.

At the same time the possibilities of redistribution of population within the Indonesian archipelago are receiving full attention from the government. Since the first days of independence, transmigration, in the sense of the planned transfer of large numbers of people from the overcrowded parts of the country to sparsely populated areas, has been envisaged as one means of facing the population problem. Unfortunately, however, the approach taken in the past was not always a realistic one for, until the First Five-Year Plan was drawn up in 1969, it tended to be based upon purely demographic considerations, though political aspects often had bearing upon specific policies and decisions. In other words, the nation's leaders and planners were inclined to think of transmigration as the way to reduce population pressure in Java. On that basis it would have been necessary to move more than 1½ million people from Java each year in order to keep pace with population increase. It has sometimes been said that transmigration has been a failure. Seen in this light, it has indeed, for in no one year in the 1950–70 period did more than 55 000 people leave Java, Madura and Bali under transmigration schemes.

Since the beginning of the First Five-Year Plan in 1969 transmigration has been placed by the government in the much wider context of regional development. Both the First and the Second Plans have placed considerable emphasis on the development of the provinces outside Java and Bali, transmigration being viewed as a means of providing support for development by increasing the mobility of labour, rather than as a way to reduce population in Java, for, as Widjojo Nitisastro has pointed out: 'a net out-migration of one million young persons annually from Java will still result in an increase in the remaining population of around 50 per cent in a thirty-year period'.[19] According to Widjojo's projections, the population of Java in 1990 will be 136 million, assuming constant fertility, rapidly declining mortality and an out-migration of 200 000 young persons annually. If it were conceivably possible to move one million young persons annually, the figure for 1990 would be 94·9 million.[20]

Whether future programmes for moving people in large numbers are successful remains to be seen, for the problems inherent in any large-scale movement of people are such that success will not be attained easily or cheaply. The most important of these problems will be examined in later chapters but first some attention should be given to the physical features that have made Java different from the other islands of the archipelago, for many of the problems met with in transmigration have had their origin in these differences, which are basically responsible for the present maldistribution of population in Indonesia.

[1] Estimate given in *Rencana Pembangunan Lima Tahun Kedua 1974/1975–1978/1979*, Department of Information (Jakarta, 1974), I, p. 79.

[2] The Central Bureau of Statistics, quoted in *Kompas*, Editorial, 27 August 1973.

[3] Widjojo Nitisastro, *Population Trends in Indonesia*, Cornell University Press (Ithaca, 1970), p. 206.

[4] *Rencana Pembangunan Lima Tahun Kedua*, op. cit., I, p. 85.

[5] Widjojo Nitisastro, op. cit., p. 220.

[6] *The Strategy of Transmigration and Co-operatives in the Context of National Strategy*, Department of Transmigration and Co-operatives (Jakarta, March 1972), p. 2. However, with a rise in national income due largely to oil exports, the per capita income in mid-1974 was placed at US$125 (*Sinar Harapan*, 26 August 1974).

[7] *Rencana Pembangunan Lima Tahun Kedua*, op. cit., I, p. 279. Petroleum products are not included in these figures for imports.

[8] Nugroho, *Indonesia, Facts and Figures*, Terbitan Pertjobaan (Jakarta, 1967), p. 235.

[9] Ibid., p. 237.

[10] See E. Utrecht, 'Land Reform in Indonesia', *Bulletin of Indonesian Economic Studies*, Vol. V, No. 3, November 1969, for a detailed discussion of implementation of the Basic Agrarian Act of 1960.

[11] A.L. McComb, 'Land Use and Area Development Problems in the Upper Solo River Basin' in *Transmigration in the Context of Area Development*, Transmigration Training and Research Centre, Department of Manpower, Transmigration and Co-operatives (Jakarta, 1974), pp. 118-24.

[12] A survey made in West Java in March 1970 showed that actual consumption of kerosene and diesel oil by the public and by industry was only 23 per cent of the estimate made by the Bureau of Statistics, which allowed 8 litres per person per month. The conclusion drawn in the survey was that a much larger quantity of wood and charcoal is still being used than estimated and that very serious destruction of forests must be taking place in this province. *The Trend Towards the Use of Solar Oil in Light Industries in West Java*, Directorate-General for Forestry (Jakarta, 1970).

[13] For a detailed discussion of the B.U.U.D. programme, which was first introduced in April 1971, see Soedarsono Hadisapoetro, 'Badan Usaha Unit Desa dan Masalah Pembinaannya' in *Prisma*, August 1973, p. 31.

[14] Rice production in 1971 (13·7 million tonnes), 1972 (13·3 million tonnes) and 1973 (14·4 million tonnes) has shown a definite increase on the 1968 figure of 11·7 million tonnes. *Rencana Pembangunan Lima Tahun Kedua*, op. cit., II, p. 19.

[15] *Rencana Pembangunan Lima Tahun Kedua*, op. cit., II, p. 435.

[16] In the census, urban areas were defined in the administrative sense as municipalities (*kotapraja*), shire (*kabupaten*) capitals, and other towns of the same level with a population of not less than 20 000.

[17] *A Blue-Print of Policies in the Implementation of Transmigration*, Directorate-General for Transmigration (Jakarta, 1972), p. 8.

[18] *Rencana Pembangunan Lima Tahun Kedua*, op. cit., I, p. 89.

[19] The period referred to is 1960–90. Widjojo Nitisastro, op. cit., p. 235.

[20] Ibid, pp. 234-5.

II
Geographical Contrasts within Indonesia

The Natural Advantages of Java

IF a general reason had to be given for the comparative failure of transmigration projects in the years between 1950 and 1968, it could be said that not enough attention was paid to the fundamental differences between Java and Bali on the one hand and the larger islands, where settlements were made, on the other. If such serious maldistribution of population as that now apparent in the Indonesian archipelago has occurred naturally, there must be significant geographical reasons for it. This is not to say that other factors like proximity to international trade routes have not been present. The existing settlement pattern throughout the archipelago has, however, been very largely determined by certain elements within the natural environment, and these elements must be taken into consideration in any plans for the guided settlement of migrants from Java and Bali in the other islands.

The basic explanation for the uneven distribution of population lies in the inherent characteristics of Indonesia's soils. Contrary to popular belief, Indonesia does not possess vast tracts of fertile land on which the abundant rainfall will make possible the cultivation of virtually any crop.[1] This erroneous view has existed for a long time, even within Indonesia itself, and it is only in the last few years that the real situation has been understood by those responsible for development in agriculture.

The very fact of the high rainfall explains, to some extent, the infertility of soils. Rapid leaching occurs in areas where rainfall is excessive; the fact that giant dipterocarps have been growing for centuries in the rain forests of the archipelago is no indication that soils are fertile in themselves. With an almost constant movement of water downward through the soil, plant nutrients are removed from the upper layers and the reddish clay known as laterite frequently forms. Nor does the fact that volcanic eruptions have taken place, and still do occur frequently, in many parts of Indonesia, provide any guarantee that soils will be fertile and suited to agriculture, once the land is cleared.

On the other hand, it is a fact that some parts of Indonesia do have remarkably fertile soils, which, despite centuries of cultivation, can still produce three crops of rice a year with virtually no fertilization. Most of these soils, however, are to be found in Java and Bali. Yet even in Java there are large areas of poor soil, supporting relatively high populations. These tend to be 'minus' areas where rural proverty is at its worst.

The reasons for this unequal distribution of good soil can be traced back to the geological origins of the archipelago. The present structure of the islands has resulted from three periods of folding which occurred on what was once, before the rise in sea-level after the last Ice Age, an extension of the South-East Asian mainland. The oldest of these movements, in geological terms, is evident in the islands of the Riau and Lingga Archipelagos, Bangka, Belitung and Karimata, and in the eroded mountains of south-western Kalimantan, all of which represent a continuation of the mountain ridges of the Malay peninsula. The second period of folding can be seen in the island of Nias and the other islands off the west coast of Sumatra, in the islands of Sumba and Timor further east, and in Seram and Buru. The third movement has caused the mountain chains of western Sumatra and southern Java, and the islands of Bali, Lombok, Sumbawa and Flores. It was along this third and most recent line of folding that Quaternary volcanoes appeared. Unfortunately, the volcanoes of Sumatra, with the notable exceptions of Marapi in West Sumatra and Sinabung and Sibayak to the west of Medan, have produced acid material that has weathered into comparatively infertile soils. In Java, on the other hand, the volcanoes have been mostly andesitic in nature and the material produced has been more basic in content. Hence the soils derived from it have always been more suited to agriculture.

Over the centuries, a very elaborately balanced system of wet-rice cultivation has developed in Java and Bali on areas of good soil, for sedentary agriculture was encouraged from early times by the nature of the soil. With apparently inexhaustible soil fertility, there was no reason for the shifting cultivation pattern to develop. A certain balance was achieved, for the soil was replenished by volcanic eruptions at fairly frequent intervals, either through deposits of volcanic ash or else by alluvium weathered from lava outpourings on the upper slopes. At the same time, leaching was not too serious, for the lowland plains and inland river basins do not receive an excessively heavy rainfall,[2] and there is a definite dry season ranging from three to five months in these parts. Flood waters have spread fresh layers of alluvium over the land frequently enough and water moving through man-made irrigation channels has helped to carry silt from the rivers to the fields themselves.

Human settlement in Java in early times was greatly facilitated by the natural terrain of the island. There are no great mountain chains to hinder movement and communications. The volcanic peaks formed on a base of Tertiary rocks that is not very high, except in the Priangan Highlands of West Java. The volcanoes, ten of which are over 3 000 m high, are well separated from each other; they appear at intervals of about 30 to 45 km and between them there are broad, well-drained areas of flat land, ideal for farming. The rivers likewise aided early human settlement by providing easy communication routes, though this function has become less important with modern progress in transportation.

The absence of very dense forest, typical of much of Sumatra, Kalimantan and Irian Jaya, where rainfall is far heavier, was a further advantage in Java. Early sedentary agriculture was helped by the fact that man was able to compete with nature in the sense that he could fell the forest trees and make permanent clearings without the harder task of removing dense jungle. Furthermore, he could keep his clearings under control; he did not have to fight constantly against encroaching secondary vegetation, for the relatively long dry season discouraged extensive growth of ground cover.

Java has always had the further advantage of having no swamps of any significance. The natural slope of the land is sufficient to permit good natural drainage, while tidal scour in the Java Sea is strong enough to carry away material brought down by the rivers. Although the coastline is gradually being extended northwards because of sedimentation, the estimated rate of 9 m per year is moderate by comparison with that of 90 m in eastern Sumatra.[3]

With the sharp rise in population during this present century, however, conditions are rapidly changing. More and more is being demanded of all soil, poor as well as fertile, and even where chemical fertilizers are now being used, together with high-productivity seeds, as part of the *Bimas* intensification programme, the limits are already obvious. As pointed out earlier, erosion and floods are increasing. At one time these two factors formed a part of the natural balance, but that stage has been passed. Natural disasters, such as the eruption of Mt. Agung in Bali in 1963, result in large numbers of people who have nowhere to go, at least within their own island, because virtually all arable land is being used. At one time, an eruption would have meant evacuation and resettlement elsewhere on the island, with a gradual return to the lava-covered land and to the arduous but rewarding task of bringing it under cultivation again. This is of course slowly happening in the Mt. Agung area. In the meantime, however, empty land is not available in Bali for the evacuees.

In any discussion of the overcrowded islands, mention must be made of the smaller islands of Madura, Bali and Lombok, all of which, although they are quite dissimilar geographically, suffer from the problem of overpopulation and a decreasing land-man ratio.

Administratively a part of the province of East Java,[4] Madura (area 5 304 sq km, population 2 385 169 in 1971) is geographically a continuation of the Pegunungan Kapur Utara (North Chalk Range) of northern Java, and hence the soils, of limestone origin, are inherently poor. The relatively flat terrain would otherwise be an asset. The island has never experienced any volcanic activity, and such fertility as soils have in a few areas is the result of wind-carried ash from the volcanoes of Java. The long dry season, usually averaging five months, places further handicaps upon farming. The Madurese, however, are extremely skilful in the terracing of dry fields and the island supports a population that averages 450 to the sq km. But the rural poverty found in some parts of Madura is possibly surpassed only by that in the Gunung Kidul area of southern Central Java.

The tiny island of Bali has an area of 5 623 sq km, much of which is occupied by a composite block of volcanoes, yet in 1971 it supported a population of 2 120 338. Geologically, it has the same structure as southern Java, with still-active volcanoes rising from a low base of Tertiary rocks. The coastal plain is relatively narrow, but the slopes of the volcanoes have been terraced with amazing skill and are cultivated as intensively as any area in the world. The consequence of the Balinese farmer's skill and perseverance has been a constantly increasing population! However, these same qualities have made the Balinese the most successful of all migrants. Today Bali cannot support any more people,

through sheer lack of land, nor can intensification be carried much further.

Lombok, along with Java, Madura and Bali, has been classed as an 'area of origin' from which migration is to be encouraged (Presidential Decree No. 1, 1973, 4 January 1973). Although this island (4 723 sq km) has a smaller population than Bali (1·6 million in 1971), it does not have the same resources of good soil and adequate water, for the limestone soils that cover the southern and eastern parts of the island and the long dry season limit agriculture. The south-eastern area is one of the few parts of Indonesia where famines occur regularly.

Sumatra and the Natural Environment

Sumatra is very different from Java in almost all its geographical features, and as a result a very different land use pattern has evolved in response to natural conditions. As far as agriculture is concerned, the main handicaps are poor soils that in most areas are well leached, terrain that does not favour settlement and communications, and broad areas of swamps.

The Bukit Barisan Ranges, which run from north to south on the western side of the island, have always proved something of a barrier to communications across Sumatra. Although many large rivers rise in these mountains and flow towards the Straits of Malacca, they do not cut right through the barrier of ranges and so have never been as important for communication purposes as those of Java. Broad stretches of swamps, located along the east coast of the island and extending as far as 150 km inland, cover about one-third of the land. They have further restricted human settlement and movement except in the provinces of Lampung, North Sumatra and Aceh. Even today, technology has not progressed to the point where profitable use can be made of these swamps, though in places where a tidal influence exists in river estuaries and tributaries, farmers have with great ingenuity established rice-fields wherein irrigation water is controlled by the rise and fall of the tides.[5] In a later chapter reference will be made to transmigration settlements established in such tidal areas.

The major problem from the farmer's point of view has been the infertility of soils throughout the greater part of Sumatra. In the foothill region to the east of the Bukit Barisan Ranges, where undulating land and the absence of swamps permit agriculture, soils have developed from the weathered material, acid in nature, produced by the volcanoes in the ranges to the west. Leaching has occurred, for most of Sumatra to the south of Medan receives a heavy rainfall.[6]

As a consequence of these features of the natural environment, a shifting form of agriculture developed in Sumatra centuries ago. Man discovered that, once the huge trees of the rain forest covering the swamp-free parts of the island were felled, the soil rapidly lost its fertility. Two or three crops in succession soon exhausted the minerals stored in the top layers of the soil. What man did not then understand was that a particular kind of balance had been achieved by nature. The leaves dropped by the trees formed humus which, when absorbed into the soil, was sufficient to maintain tree growth. With the removal of the trees, the source of humus and hence of soil nutrients was removed and this, coupled with leaching that increased with the removal of vegetative cover, meant a rapid decline in fertility. Faced with such a situation, the cultivator had no choice but to move from his clearing and begin the whole process over again. These abandoned clearings soon became covered in secondary growth that was particularly dense for, with the removal of the large trees that had once shaded the soil, sunlight could reach right down to the ground. In much of Sumatra and some parts of Kalimantan, the consequence has been large areas of *alang-alang* grass (*Imperata cylindrica*), which is even harder to remove than virgin forest.

In fact, the pattern of shifting agriculture that developed in Sumatra and, less extensively, in other parts of the archipelago with a similar natural environment, represented an adjustment made by man to his environment. He could not alter his surroundings, as he did in Java with the introduction of irrigated rice-fields, and so he worked out for himself a way of life that brought about no permanent disruption in the ecological balance achieved by nature. Shifting agriculture is usually regarded as a destructive and wasteful form of land use because it gives rise to the growth of *alang-alang* and other kinds of secondary vegetation. But in the past it was the only way that man could come to terms with nature in areas such as Sumatra. Today, it is the policy of the Indonesian government to limit shifting agriculture and to convert this form of land utilization to something more economically beneficial. While this objective is undoubtedly a good one, since Indonesia's high population makes optimum use of all land resources essential, it is not an easy thing to convert such land to sedentary agriculture, as many transmigration projects in the past have discovered to their cost.

Kalimantan, Sulawesi and Irian Jaya

Most of the problems evident in Sumatra can be seen in Kalimantan also, though there is one significant difference in the geological background to present-day conditions. There has been no recent vulcanism at all and leaching has occurred so extensively that soils today offer few attractions to the ordinary cultivator. As in Sumatra, rainfall tends to be excessive,[7] and the 'dry' season is not so much a rainless time as a period of less rain. It remains to be seen to what extent the use of chemical fertilizers can alter the situation here and in other parts of the archipelago.

The terrain, too, has not encouraged human settlement. Here, more than in any part of Indonesia except Irian Jaya, the rivers are important as communication routes, though navigation in some cases is restricted by rapids and sand-bars. Human settlement is still virtually limited to the land close to the river banks. The mountains of Kalimantan are not high but they are rugged enough to make road-building difficult and expensive. The fact that population is sparse and scattered means that money spent on road construction is not really a good economic investment.

The real obstacle to development has always been the unhealthy swamps that extend along the western and southern coasts of the island. Poor drainage has resulted in large areas of permanent swamp, as well as even greater areas of seasonal swamps. Given all these conditions which are similar to those of Sumatra, a similar type of shifting agriculture has developed, though on the whole it is less technically advanced. In many parts of interior Kalimantan, people still depend for their livelihood upon the gathering of forest products like rattan, resins, and *tengkawang* seeds.[8]

Sulawesi has some of the same problems as those in Sumatra and Kalimantan, though perhaps the most serious is the scarcity of flat land for agriculture. It is an island of uplands, cut by deep rift valleys. The coastal plains are negligible in size, and farming land is virtually limited to certain parts of the southern peninsulas. The block structure of the mountains has always hindered communications; it is easier to travel from one place to another by boat, across the gulfs that separate the peninsulas from one another, than by land. Once again, there has been no recent vulcanism, except for the area around Ujung Pandang (formerly Makassar) and a small district at the tip of the northern peninsula. Soils are infertile, having been formed from non-basic parent rock, and leaching has occurred, although there is a fairly long dry season.[9] In fact, lack of water in the dry season has always restricted agriculture in the flatter and more fertile areas of the island. On the other hand, the block nature of the island's structure and the very deep seas around the peninsulas have prevented the formation of swamps, except in a few limited areas. Despite the many disadvantages of Sulawesi, two of the most successful of all transmigration areas are to be found in the Parigi and Luwu districts.

Irian Jaya may be said to have every disadvantage existing elsewhere in the archipelago, though on a far greater scale. The Central Ranges, in which Mt. Jaya rises to 5 030 m and ten peaks are permanently snow-covered, cut the island from west to east. Huge rivers, rising in these ranges, flow to the north, while somewhat shorter ones flow to the south, but none provides a real communication route to the interior of the island. The people of the uplands live in virtual isolation, whilst those to the north and south of the mountain barrier are effectively cut off from each other. The waterfalls and rapids found in most of the rivers restrict navigation, except within limited areas.

There has been no recent volcanic activity in Irian Jaya, except in the area around Mt. Umsini. Consequently soils are poor and have also experienced serious leaching, for most of the island receives excessively heavy rainfall.[10] Forest vegetation, similar to that found in most of Sumatra and Kalimantan, has developed, but man has not adjusted to this natural environment to the extent that he has in Sumatra.

The shifting cultivator in Sumatra grows dry rice and often plants rubber trees to be tapped in later years, before he abandons his clearing. He is aware of the possibilities of a cash economy. But in Irian Jaya, the shifting cultivator often depends more upon hunting and gathering than upon cultivation of crops, which is secondary to the collection of sago in many parts of the province.[11] As a consequence, the traces of shifting cultivation, in the form of *alang-alang* and secondary forest, are less apparent and Irian Jaya has the highest percentage of original forest cover within the archipelago.

Regional Development Today

Today, when serious thought is being given to the transfer of some of Java's population to other parts of the country, it is obviously the islands of Sumatra, Kalimantan and Sulawesi that are the most relevant, for the distance alone of Irian Jaya from Java makes transmigration expensive. But equally obviously, the frame of reference for any plans involving agricultural settlements and land development projects must be different, for there are few basic similarities between the islands from which migration is necessary and the other large islands of the archipelago.

Regional development involves the utilization of resources located in the various provinces, which means agricultural expansion and also the development of mining and forestry activities. To concentrate on the latter without proper development of existing agricultural potential would be to encourage the existing lack of balance between Java and the other islands.

Transmigration settlements in the past have often not been very successful, and in many instances have been complete failures, because planners have, in their preoccupation with the wet-rice pattern of farming typical of Java, remained unaware of the agricultural potential offered by these parts of the archipelago for the cultivation of crops other than rice. The Dutch colonial government, in its colonization schemes, had concentrated on projects with irrigated rice as the major product,[12] and the same basic policy was continued after independence by the Indonesian government. Those responsible for planning settlements have attempted to establish in a matter of two or three years the same pattern of agriculture and the same agrarian economy that took centuries to develop in the very different physical environment of Java. Therefore, it is not at all surprising that failures have occurred, failure being interpreted not by the actual numbers of people moved from Java but by the extent to which the individual migrant has been able to obtain a better standard of living as a consequence of his labours.

Wet-rice cultivation is not the only form of agriculture that can support a rural population in the tropics. The fact that soil and terrain have not favoured sedentary agriculture based upon rice growing does not mean that there are no agricultural possibilities in the islands other than Java and Bali. The progress made in the production of chemical fertilizers suggests that many of the poorer soils of these islands may be capable of producing both food and non-food crops in a profitable way, and it has been shown in Lampung that deep ploughing, using machinery, can destroy the roots of *alang-alang* in a way that ordinary hoeing cannot. In most parts of Sumatra, the number of smallholdings producing rubber, pepper and coffee has increased steadily in the last twenty years. The real possibilities for dry farming have as yet not been fully investigated. Similarly, no attention has been given to prospects for large-scale animal husbandry. It has long been accepted that cattle breeding must be limited to the very dry parts of East Nusatenggara, yet in Sulawesi, animal husbandry could certainly be developed, if detailed studies were made of existing conditions and of progress already achieved in other tropical areas like northern Australia.[13]

Quite apart from agricultural possibilities, there are also possibilities for forestry undertakings, for the islands outside Java and Bali are still very largely covered in their original forest vegetation. There are equally good opportunities for the cultivation of man-made forests of soft woods.[14] In a world demanding ever-increasing supplies of paper, Indonesia could grow soft woods very rapidly, with the help of the heavy rainfall and the high temperatures. But labour is required for all such undertakings, and it is in this context that transmigration projects can be very significant.

The same applies to mining, which is becoming more and more important in the Indonesian economy.[15] Although Java is well endowed with fertile soil, it is noticeably poor in minerals. The other islands, however, all contain minerals of one kind or another, often for the very reasons that have deprived them of good soil. Although the actual work of mining is heavily mechanized, there are many associated activities, such as road construction and the cultivation of food crops to supply mining camps, that require labour.

Regional development is undoubtedly essential for overall national development. A better balance in population distribution is likewise necessary, if labour is to be made available for new undertakings that will stimulate economic growth in the provinces outside Java. The problem is how to set about organizing migration on a sufficiently large scale. As in all cases, much can be learned from the experiences and mistakes of the past. The problems that hindered the successful implementation of transmigration in the years between 1950 and 1968 should be looked at carefully because of their bearing upon present policies and programmes.

[1] C.A. Fisher, *South-east Asia* Methuen (London, 1964), p. 50.

[2] Average annual rainfall (1931–60): Jakarta–1 760 mm (69·3"); Semarang–2 033 mm (80"); Surabaya–1 518 mm (59·8"); Yogyakarta–2 002 mm (78·8"). *Statistical Pocketbook of Indonesia 1964–1967*, Central Bureau of Statistics (Jakarta, January 1968), p. 6.

[3] Soekmono gives a very good description of the sedimentation process that has been taking place over the centuries in eastern Sumatra and northern Java in 'Geomorphology and the Location of Sriwijaya' in *Madjalah Ilmu-ilmu Sastra Indonesia*, April 1963 (pp. 79-92) and 'A Geographical Reconstruction of Northeastern Central Java and the Location of Medang' in *Indonesia* No. 4, October 1967, pp. 2-7.

[4] In all statistics, Madura is included in the province of East Java.

[5] *Program, Progress & Prospek*, Project for the Opening of Tidal Rice-Fields, Directorate-General for Water Resources, Department of Public Works and Power (Jakarta (no date)), p. 18.

[6] Average annual rainfall (1931–60): Medan–2 053 mm (80·8") Pekanbaru–2 576 mm (101·4"); Jambi–3 099 mm (122"); Palembang–2 381 mm (93·7"). *Statistical Pocketbook of Indonesia 1964–1967*, op. cit., p. 6.

[7] Average annual rainfall (1931–60): Pontianak–3 056 mm (120"); Banjarmasin–2 755 mm (108·5"); Samarinda–2 088 mm (82·2"). *Statistical Pocketbook of Indonesia 1964–1967*, op. cit., p. 6.

[8] The seeds of a certain tree, used in the making of cosmetics and of chocolate because of their oil content.

[9] Average annual rainfall (1931–60): Ujung Pandang–3 188 mm (125·5"); Manado–3 352 mm (132"). *Statistical Pocketbook of Indonesia 1964–1967*, op. cit., p. 6.

[10] Rainfall in 1966: Biak–3 382 mm (133"); Jayapura–2 274 mm (89·5"). *Statistical Pocketbook of Indonesia 1970 & 1971*, Central Bureau of Statistics (Jakarta, August 1972), pp. 9 and 10.

[11] Koentjaraningrat and H.W. Bachtiar, (ed.), *Penduduk Irian Barat*, P.T. Penerbitan Universitas (Jakarta, 1963), p. 139 and p. 253.

[12] Many years ago, Karl Pelzer pointed out that settlement of Javanese farmers outside Java should not seek to copy the pattern of agricultural life found in Java. Karl J. Pelzer, *Pioneer Settlement in the Asiatic Tropics*, Institute of Pacific Relations (New York, 1945), p. 230.

[13] The project, financed by the World Bank to develop cattle breeding in South Sulawesi, is worth noting.

[14] It is intended that the Takengon paper mill in Aceh will use the fast-growing *pinus Merkusii*, cultivated locally, for pulp purposes.

[15] Exports of petroleum and other minerals rose from US$446 million in 1969–70 to an estimated US$1 880 million in 1973–4. *Rencana Pembangunan Lima Tahun Kedua*, op. cit., I, p. 275.

III

Transmigration Policies

Dutch Colonization Policies

THE census taken by the Dutch colonial government in 1905 showed that 30 million people were living in Java and Madura, with only 7½ million in the other islands of the East Indies. The Dutch were already conscious of the fact that steps should be taken to improve the welfare of the ordinary farmer in Java; the Ethical Policy,[1] introduced in the years immediately after 1900, reflected a rather belated awareness that the forced changes introduced into the indigenous farming economy of Java by colonial policies meant steadily decreasing living standards for the people of the island.

In the first years of the twentieth century, the Dutch colonial government commenced what was described as a 'colonization' policy, the aim being to establish 'colonies' of settlers from Java in the other islands. This new policy was motivated to a certain extent by the desire to relieve population pressure in Java, but the Dutch government was undoubtedly aware of the advantages that could be gained in later years from a larger supply of labour in the other islands of the archipelago, particularly in Sumatra. It was surely no coincidence that interest in moving farmers from the rural parts of Java appeared at the time when foreign companies were beginning to establish plantations in Sumatra. Professor Anwas Adiwilaga, speaking at the 1970 Transmigration Seminar, summed up this aspect when he said: 'It was only after Dutch entrepreneurs spread their wings to islands other than Java, specially Sumatra, that the Government of the Dutch Indies saw the need for a supply of cheap coolie labour in those islands.'[2]

Most of the Dutch settlements were made in the residency of Lampung in southern Sumatra, and by far the greater percentage of people, moved to colonization settlements between 1905 and 1941, went to that area, where three major projects were established: Gedong Tataan, Kota Agung and Sukadana.

In 1905, 155 families were settled in the Gedong Tataan district and, as more people were transferred each year, more land was opened up and new villages were established. The land chosen was reasonably fertile and well-watered and by 1911 there were 6 073 people in the new settlement, which was regarded as a successful but expensive undertaking.[3]

These first migrants had been given everything required for an agricultural settlement with an allocation of one hectare of land per family, but because of the expense involved the system was altered in 1912. Migrants then received free transport from their place of origin, plus a sum of money to pay off debts in their home village. Land was given free in Lampung, but the settlers had to repay money lent by the government for the purchase of housing materials, tools and seed to the Lampongsche Volksbank, which had been established in 1911 to assist in the financing of colonization settlements.

By the end of 1921, there were 19 572 people in the villages around Gedong Tataan. Since there was by then a shortage of suitable land in this area, another site was selected close to Kota Agung. In 1922, 2 720 people were placed there in the village of Wonosobo, and a certain number moved to the new settlement from the overcrowded villages of the Gedong Tataan district.

Meanwhile attention had been given to other parts of southern Sumatra. In 1909 migrants were placed at Kepahiang in the Rejang district of Bengkulu. Further settlements were made between 1911 and 1919 in the Lebong district, many of the settlers being contract labourers who, having finished their contracts, became smallholder coffee-growers, producing just enough food crops for their own needs, as the local people of the area did. A small settlement of former plantation labourers was established at Pagar Alam in the Palembang residency, but an attempt made in 1919 to settle people at Mata Lintang in the same residency failed completely, as did an attempt in 1921 to settle 250 families near Barabai in Kalimantan.

In the years between 1923 and 1931, the only migrants moved from Java by the government were the 1 693 people placed in the Gedong Tataan area in 1928, though during this period quite a number of people moved of their own accord to the two settlements in Lampung. Those moved in 1928 by the government were given only free transport and land; on arrival in Lampung they had to rely on the goodwill of earlier settlers for help with tools, housing and so on.

Government interest in colonization had declined, partly because of attempts to reduce government expenditure and partly because of trouble within the Lampongsche Volksbank itself. Crop failures in the Kota Agung area, which was not as well suited to agriculture as the Gedong Tataan area, made it impossible for settlers to repay their debts to the Bank. At the same time, the Bank itself was not well controlled and hence it was closed in 1928, its debts being taken over by the government.

In 1930, for the first time, some villages, totalling nine altogether, were handed over to the civil administration of the residency of Lampung. Gedong Tataan became a *kecamatan* (District), and land titles were given to a certain number of the older settlers.

In 1932 the Dutch government decided to resume colonization, the provision of a source of potential plantation workers undoubtedly influencing policies now that labour conditions were beginning to change. Up to this time, plantations had obtained labour by arranging for the recruitment and transporta-tion of workers on contract for a certain number of years. But the gradual removal of the 'penal sanction', contained in the Coolie Ordinance,[4] meant that in the years after 1930 a shortage of labour would seriously hinder further expansion of the plantations that had proved so profitable in the north-eastern part of Sumatra. The availability of farm labour, not too far from these planta-tions and from the plantations of southern Sumatra, would be a great advantage.[5]

Thus approximately 7 000 migrants were sent to Lampung in 1932, a few being placed in the Kota Agung area but most going to Gedong Dalam, a new village established in the Sukadana district of Central Lampung. After this proved successful, it was decided to establish a large-scale settlement at Sukadana, although small settlements were also made in areas occupied by the indigenous people of Lampung and normally located close to existing plantations. In 1930, 1931 and 1932, more settlements were made in Bengkulu, but they were very small, less than 1 000 people all told being involved.

With the resumption of colonization in 1932, a new policy was adopted. Settlers already established for some years in the two older settlements had been feeling the need of additional farm labour at harvest time, for, with improvements in irrigation, they were obtaining good yields from their rice-fields. Making use of the traditional Javanese system of employing labourers to help with the harvest in return for a share of the crop, known as the *upah bawon* or 'wage for help with the harvest', the government transported prospective settlers, in many cases the rela-tives or friends of established migrants, to southern Lampung shortly before harvest time. The old migrants gave the newcomers accommodation and food in their own homes for 3 to 6 weeks, plus a wage in the form of between one-seventh and one-fifth of the rice crop, in return for their help in harvesting.[6]

This new method, tried first in 1932, was used again when, in 1934, 1 375 people were moved to the Gedong Tataan area, where the adult migrants worked as *bawon* labourers. After harvest time, most of these newcomers were shifted to the new villages already planned by the government in the Sukadana area, where water was available for irrigation from the Way Sekampung[7] after the construction of the Argoguruh Weir. As the Sukadana villages began to expand, the *bawon* system was used to bring more migrants into the area (see Table 3).

The *bawon* system had certain advantages from the government's point of view in that it was cheap and greatly facilitated adjustment of the individual farmer to his new environment. The government gave only land and transport; food for the first few months, when the new migrant was clearing and bringing under cultivation the piece of land given

Table 3
Number of Migrants in Colonization Settlements in Lampung, 1905–1941

Period	Government-sponsored migrants	Total number at end of year
1905–1911	–[1]	6 073
1912–1922	16 838	22 274
1923–1933[2]	8 693	37 257
1934	1 375	37 477
1935	12 524	51 605
1936	12 181	62 764
1937	14 938	73 499
1938	20 014	91 595
1939	27 826	120 464
1940	31 173	144 619
1941	35 251	173 959

Source: Compiled from data in Amral Sjamsu, op.cit., p. 9.

Notes: [1] Details are not available for the number moved in this period; the figure would be somewhat less than 6 073, which includes those born in settlements and those moving of their own accord.
[2] In this period migrants were moved only in 1928 and 1932; the increase in end-of-year figures is the result of natural increase and the arrival of independent migrants.

to him, was guaranteed by the rice he had obtained as his *upah bawon*. In time, however, the number of prospective migrants exceeded the number needed to help harvest the crops of earlier settlers. Also, only those with a small number of dependants could migrate under this system, for, if a man had too many children, he could not feed them all on the rice received in return for labour.

An adaptation of this system was introduced in 1937, when the government made use of the *keluarga* or family system. This resembled the *bawon* system, which still continued to operate, in that established settlers sponsored people from Java. The newcomers lived with them while preparing their land and building houses. But they were not actually employed in the way that *bawon* labourers were. The new migrants were given land but had to repay other money, including transportation, made available to help them get established in the new villages. Only a limited number of people could be moved in this way since only a certain number of people wanted to sponsor relatives, who could be a greater and more permanent burden than actual *bawon* labourers.

With the expansion of the Sukadana settlement, the migrant population of Lampung continued to rise, although from 1935 onwards new settlers had to repay all money spent for transportation, housing and other purposes. The central village of the area soon developed into the town known after 1937 as Metro. In 1941, the Sukadana area had about 90 000 of the 173 959 people who had moved into the residency under colonization schemes or who had been born in the settlements of migrant parents. This was the most successful of all colonization projects in the archipelago, though the term 'successful' should be interpreted in a very limited sense. The comparative prosperity of this area stemmed from the fact that the site was well chosen from the point of view of both soil and water. Irrigation was made available in the first years of the settlement though migrants who wished to settle in the area had to give 75 days of labour (15 days in the first year and 30 in each of the second and third years) to the construction of irrigation facilities.[8]

In the late 1930s, attention was given to other parts of Sumatra, and to the other less populated islands (see Table 4). In 1937, a successful settlement was established at Belitang, with a much smaller one at Tugumulyo, in the Palembang residency; the two settlements were expensive for the government, however, since the *bawon* system could not be used. More migrants were placed in the Bengkulu residency, where a new settlement was established at Kemumu. Here it was possible to use the *bawon* system, as there were already well-established, though relatively small, settlements in the area. Two small settlements were made at Tabir in Jambi (1940) and at Batahan in West Sumatra (1941). In the case of the former, harvests were so bad that food had to be given free to the settlers by the government.

In the years between 1937 and 1941 six settlements were established in Sulawesi. The settlement at Paria on the western side of the

Table 4
Number of Migrants in Colonization Settlements throughout Indonesia, end of 1940

Area	Total population in settlements
Residency of Lampung	144 619[1]
Residency of Palembang	19 876
Residency of Bengkulu	7 443
Jambi and West Sumatra	1 920
Kalimantan	3 107
Sulawesi	23 600
	200 565

Source: Compiled from data in Amral Sjamsu, op. cit., pp. 9, 50, 55, 56, 61 and 66.

[1] The figure for Lampung had risen to 173,959 by the end of 1941.

south-western peninsula did not develop satisfactorily, mainly because of lack of irrigation, but the Mapili settlement (1937) in the same district grew rapidly. A small settlement made on the island of Muna, off the south-eastern peninsula, was a failure due to bad selection of the site.

The other settlements—Bone-Bone/Masamba (1938), Kalaena (1938) and Lamasi (1940)—were located on the Luwu plain at the northern end of the Gulf of Bone and were by far the most successful of the Dutch colonization projects in Sulawesi. The area was relatively underpopulated and settlers encountered no problems over land claims by local inhabitants. At the end of 1940 there were 16 628 people in the Luwu settlements. The fact that several rivers flow across the plain made possible the construction of irrigation facilities very soon after the settlements were established. Although work on technical irrigation networks stopped with the outbreak of the Second World War, the Javanese settlers were able to extend the partly completed canal system with village-style channels.

In Kalimantan two settlements were established, Madurejo (1938) and Purwosari (1939). The former, as its name implies, was founded by people from Madura; it depended upon dry farming, with which the Madurese settlers were quite familiar. The latter, in a swamp area on the Tamban River near Banjarmasin, was based upon the cultivation of irrigated rice; the migrants from Java were first trained in the techniques of rice growing in tidal areas at two training centres set up for this purpose in southern Kalimantan.

Any attempt to sum up the achievements of the Dutch colonization undertakings must take into consideration the aims involved. If it is assumed that the purpose was to relieve population pressure in Java, obviously very little was achieved, for the number of people in colonization settlements (including those who had moved into settlement areas without government assistance and those born in the settlements) was only 200 565 at the end of 1940. This was a mere fraction of the increase in Java between 1905 and 1940. Although numbers of migrants continued to rise each year, the number moved in 1941 was less than one-twentieth of the increase in Java in that year. From the point of view of population growth in the other islands, however, colonization did have some effect in Lampung, where the total population of the residency, estimated at about 511 400 in 1941, consisted of only 215 000 indigenous people and more than a quarter of a million people from different parts of Java.[9]

From the point of view of living standards of the new settlers, very little was really achieved and the outward appearance of prosperity disguised the fact that economically the individual farmer even in the Sukadana district, the 'best' of all the Dutch settlement areas, was not really much better off than his relatives back in Java. Fisher has pointed out the basic reason for this.

In all cases the authorities strove to preserve as much as possible of the Javan pattern of agriculture in the new settlements, and colonists usually received one hectare of land (2·47 acres) per family to be used solely for subsistence crops.[10]

In retaining the same pattern of subsistence agriculture found in Java, the Dutch colonization authority, perhaps unwittingly, made possible the development of many of the problems of rural Java. Insufficient land was left for the expansion of settlements and even in the 1930s settlements in the Gedong Tataan and the Kota Agung areas were overcrowded. The fragmentation of holdings, so much a feature of rural Java, has occurred in these two areas and in the Sukadana district also. Today the average holding is closer to half a hectare than to one hectare. Buying and selling of holdings has also taken place and land has tended to accumulate in the hands of a limited number of people. Population density in the Sukadana settlement was already 342 per sq km in 1941; the fact that the Indonesian transmigration authority continued to settle people in and around this area during the 1950s has made the situation worse.

The problem of rural indebtedness, found in much of Java, reappeared in the Dutch settlements. The *ijon* system was present even in colonial times, with settlers selling their rice before harvest time to private rice-mills that were, in most cases, Chinese-owned. The colonial government became aware of this problem in the years immediately preceding the Japanese occupation and had taken steps to try to restrict the economic power of the rice-mills.[11] But it is no easy task to do away with the *ijon* system, as post-independence authorities have discovered in Java. No attempt was made in the Dutch settlements to encourage co-operative action among farmers to enable them to obtain credit or to market their products more profitably. The further fact that no attempt was made to establish any kind of industry, even small home industries connected with processing of agricultural products, made the farmer completely dependent on what he harvested from his fields.

Another aspect, related also to the fact that only a very small piece of land was given to migrants, has been the inability of farmers to grow cash crops. The basic assumption was that the traditional wet-rice pattern of Java would be continued; diversification in the cropping pattern was not considered. Hence when a bad season has occurred and rice yields have been low, the settlers have had nothing to fall back on. The indigenous people of the areas around settlements, with their rubber and pepper gardens, have always been in a better economic position. Where newcomers from Java were able to combine the cultivation of food crops like dry rice and cassava with the cultivation of cash crops, a rise in incomes occurred fairly rapidly. But such cases are to be found in the smaller settlements of Bengkulu and not in the large-scale, irrigated settlements of South and Central

Lampung, or in the plantation-oriented settlements of the northern part of Lampung, where migrants were deliberately given extremely small holdings so that they would be forced to work on nearby pepper plantations. These migrants could not develop into smallholders themselves since they were obliged to use all of their small piece of land for food crops.

One of the strongest criticisms of Dutch colonization, from the Indonesian point of view, has been the lack of assimilation between the newcomers from Java and the indigenous people of the settlement areas. The Dutch government established enclaves of Javanese settlers, except in Luwu, where assimilation was made much easier by the fact that the area had a very small indigenous population. To avoid the conflicts that often occurred over land in the smaller settlements, the government excluded the three big settlements in Lampung from *marga* relations.[12] To do this the government had the land transferred from the local *marga* to the colonization authority before any settlement work was commenced. The new villages were thus placed outside the authority of local traditional law and made subject to ordinary government bodies. Land owned by indigenous people within the boundaries of the big settlement areas was purchased by the government to prevent land disputes. But the introduction of the village administration pattern of Java in the colonization settlements made any sort of integration impossible. The cultural patterns of Java were maintained and the settlers had no occasion to come in contact with the cultural traditions of the areas in which they had come to live. It has been accurately pointed out that

... integration with local communities was hindered by socio-cultural barriers that had been erected by the deliberate encouragement of traditional provincial ways of life. The village community in a colonisation area remained a static agrarian community, living cut off from the society of the settlement area.[13]

In a few instances the Dutch government moved a whole village, presumably in the hope that adjustment to the new environment in Sumatra would be made easier. This policy, however, did not produce any better results for it meant that the elements that held back progress in Java were moved with the village. Although the inclusion of village craftsmen was an advantage, the new settlement had to carry the burden of comparatively large numbers of non-productive people (elderly and sick relatives and small children) as well as that of less enterprising villagers whose lack of enthusiasm and initiative proved a handicap. It is not surprising that the newcomers were, on the whole, greeted with resentment and even open hostility in some places and that the indigenous people of the various colonization areas, with the exception of Luwu, tended to show contempt towards settlers in government projects. From the point of view of the colonial government, which had no interest in encouraging unity among the different groups of people, this was no doubt an insignificant aspect of the whole undertaking. From the point of view of the overall development of southern Sumatra in particular, much more could have been achieved if the newcomers had been better assimilated.

The arrival of the Japanese in the Indonesian archipelago in 1942 put an end to all colonization projects.[14] Most of the settlements already established suffered considerably during the three years of occupation; in many cases farmers were taken from colonization villages to provide labour for Japanese war works. The Dutch government had been intending to continue its colonization programme, for large areas of land in Sumatra and Sulawesi had been surveyed during 1940 and 1941 and plans had been prepared for new settlements. The Second World War, however, meant more than the end of colonization, for with the proclamation of Indonesian independence on 17 August 1945, the colonial era came to an end.

The Post-independence Transmigration Authority

In the years immediately following the end of the Second World War, while Indonesia was still involved in the war of independence against the Dutch,[15] thoughts were already being given to plans for the resettlement of people from Java and Bali in other parts of the country. The *Panitia Siasat Ekonomi* (Committee for Economic Strategies), set up in 1947 to consider matters connected with the national economy, gave some consideration to transmigration, as the colonization programme was now called.[16] Nothing could be done, however, because of the state of war at the time. Transmigration was first placed under the Ministry of Labour and Social Welfare in 1947; it was then shifted to the Ministry of Development and Youth and later, in 1948, to the Ministry of Home Affairs. In 1950, after the transfer of sovereignty, transmigration came under the Ministry of Community Development as a Service, but when this ministry was done away with in October of the same year transmigration was transferred to the Ministry of Social Welfare. In 1957 it became the responsibility of a Minister of State for Transmigration Affairs.

With the changes in governmental structure that followed the Presidential Decree of 5 July 1959,[17] transmigration was combined with the attempt to set up co-operatives and to develop rural communities through the new Department of Transmigration, Co-operatives and Rural Community Development (Presidential Decree No. 21 of 1960). The emphasis placed by the government of the time on the growing co-operative movement and the comparative lack of interest in transmigration was reflected in the change of name of the department in 1962, when it became the Department of Co-operatives (Presidential Decree No. 99 of 1962), transmigration affairs being relegated to a Transmigration Service established within this department.

In 1963 (Presidential Decree No. 232), the name of this department was changed again to the Department of Transmigration, Co-operatives and Rural Community Development, in which there were four directorates to handle transmigration, land opening/clearing, co-operatives and rural community development. In 1964 (Presidential Decree No. 215) there was a further change, with the removal of Rural Community Development from the department. The department became the Department of Transmigration and Co-operatives and consisted of the Directorates for Co-operatives, Land Opening, Mobilization and Settlement, and Consolidation of Development in Transmigrant Communities.

In 1966, after the political upheavals of 1965, further fundamental changes occurred in the departmental structure. Transmigration was transferred to the Department of Home Affairs where it was combined with agrarian affairs to form the Directorate-General for Agrarian Affairs and Transmigration (Presidential Decree No. 173 of 1966). A further change, reflecting government policies in this period, led to a transfer of transmigration in 1967 to the Department of Veterans, which was then renamed the Department of Transmigration, Veterans and Demobilisation (Departemen Transved, Presidential Decree No. 259 of 1967). In June 1968 this department became the Department of Transmigration and Co-operatives, an arrangement that lasted until 1 April 1973, when the department was combined with the Department of Labour under the name of the Department of Manpower, Transmigration and Co-operatives. Each of the three sections has the status of a Directorate-General, under the authority of a Director-General who is responsible to the Minister for Manpower, Transmigration and Co-operatives.

From what has been said above, it is understandable that policies changed frequently in the years between 1950 and the beginning of the First Five-Year Development Plan (April 1969), depending upon the policies of the department under which transmigration happened to be placed. These frequent alterations were basically a reflection of the lack of political orientation and stability during the first twenty-five years of independence. They also reflect the fact that government views about the importance of transmigration and its relation to other government institutions altered frequently.

From the beginning, the need for some kind of channelling institution to handle transmigration matters was recognized. It was felt that migration from Java was essential and that some government body should be made responsible for encouraging and organizing it. Any evaluation of the extent to which transmigration undertakings in this period (1950–68) were successful has to be made in the context of the policies that existed at the time when the projects concerned were established and when the general concept was that Java's population problems could be solved by a transfer of people to the other islands of Indonesia. The fact that no government department in the early years of independence knew much about the process of planned migration and resettlement work meant that early policies kept more or less to those of the Dutch colonial government.

If an examination is made of the policies followed in transmigration in this early period, the most striking feature is the extremely unrealistic targets. In 1952 the Transmigration Service began the implementation of a fifteen-year Transmigration Plan originally prepared in 1947 with the aim of moving 31 million people. This plan had been reformulated in 1951, the intention being to cover the thirty-five year period from 1953 to 1987. The aim was to move 48 675 000 people during those years; in the first five years one million people plus the natural increase in those five years were to be moved, in the second five-year period 2 million people plus the natural increase in those years, in the next five-year period 3 million people plus natural increase, and so on.[18] However, very little was done about implementation and the numbers of people moved in those years, when the Dutch policy

of 'family' migration was continued, were small.

In 1953 a plan was made to shift 100 000 people in that year but once again implementation did not keep up with intentions, and only 40 009 people were moved (Table 5). The number of people moved in 1954 was even smaller and the Transmigration Service then drew up a new five-year transmigration programme as part of the Five-Year Development Plan for 1956–1960; the target for numbers to be moved during the five-year period was placed at 2 million. Although details of locations to which migrants were to be sent were prepared, implementation was far below the target. In the section dealing with transmigration in the Five-Year Plan, the problem of interdepartmental co-ordination, which has always presented a major difficulty, was stated clearly:

As a consequence (of lack of co-ordination) the Transmigration Service has itself undertaken tasks that are really included in the spheres of other Services, such as construction of roads and water channels, soil surveys, various matters connected with health and education, and so on.[19]

Despite the fact that this basic problem was recognized, nothing was done to overcome it.

An eight-year transmigration plan was then formulated as part of the Eight-Year Plan for Overall National Development which was to guide the national economy in the 1961–9 period. In referring to the achievements of the preceding decade, limited as they were by comparison with expectations, the Plan stated that:

... the failure now experienced is due to the fact that what has been taking place up to the present is merely agricultural transmigration. ... Therefore a radical change is considered necessary, namely, transmigration should follow the course of regional development outside Java in the fields of industry, mining, fisheries, plantations, and so on.[20]

Policy in selection of migrants and of locations for projects was supposed to be directed towards the supply of manpower for specific

Table 5
Number of Migrants by Area of Origin, 1950–1968

Year	West Java	Central Java	Yogya-karta	East Java	Bali	Local[1]	Total[4]
1950							77[5]
1951	69	1 588	390	502		402	2 951
1952	409	8 777	2 745	4 992		682	17 605
1953	3 028	12 754	4 427	14 751	1 054	3 995	40 009
1954	5 362	9 397	3 236	7 552	2 706	1 485[2]	29 738
1955	3 164	6 472	1 954	5 454	203	4 142	21 389
1956	3 236	9 700	2 724	8 116[3]		574	24 350
1957	1 935	7 653	2 094	4 739	497	6 312	23 230
1958	1 336	9 388	5 895	5 567	1 023	3 210	26 419
1959	5 991	15 311	2 654	14 514	3 948	3 678	46 096
1960	2 180	7 062	1 960	6 910		3 963	22 075
1961	5 109	8 470	1 363	4 317		350	19 609
1962	3 028	9 973	1 647	5 446		2 035	22 129
1963	837	4 622	695	3 138	22 598	269	32 159
1964	683	7 819	4 675	59	1 986		15 222
1965	4 202	26 524	7 503	13 803	1 193		53 225
1966	1 357	1 191	410	1 147	543		4 648
1967	2 277	3 726	653	1 770	1 140		9 566
1968	3 123	5 448	1 554	3 077	681		13 883

Source: 1950–1955, Directorate-General for Trans-migration.
1956–1968, *Statistical Pocketbooks of Indonesia*, 1957 to 1970–1.

Notes: [1] The term 'local' refers to people moving within the same province.
[2] This figure includes 1 012 people repatriated from Surinam.

[3] Figures given for East Java for 1956, 1960, 1961 and 1962 include migrants from Bali.
[4] This table does not include the 17 837 families resettled in southern Sumatra between 1950 and 1954 by the Bureau for National Reconstruction (BRN) and the Bureau for Settlement of Ex-service-men.

[5] Area of origin is not recorded.

undertakings of a developmental nature that would be planned and carried out by other government departments and by private companies. However, where farming settlements were established, irrigation was to form the basis of the economy.[21] The Plan also stated that with this new policy 'the finance required by the Transmigration Service is limited to the recruitment, accommodation and transportation of manpower'.[22] All expenses involved in settling the migrants in the new locations, including land clearing, provision of houses, and supply of food, would be borne by the project requiring the labour.

However, transmigration in fact continued to be carried out exactly as it had been during the 1950s. Most migrants came from farming areas in Java and Bali and were placed in settlements where agriculture was to form the source of livelihood, the assumption (by both the migrants themselves and the transmigration authority) being that irrigation would be made available by the Department of Public Works. A series of Joint Ministerial Decisions was issued in 1961, the intention being to follow up the policies outlined in the Eight-Year Plan. An attempt was made to establish better co-ordination between the Department of

Agriculture and the Department of Transmigration, Co-operatives and Rural Community Development (No. 62a/KMP/1961, No. 121) and between the latter and the Department of Agrarian Affairs (No. SK 982/KA, 1961, No. 113) and to formulate a 'common blue-print of basic policies' for Agrarian Affairs and Transmigration, Co-operatives and Rural Community Development (No. SK 404/KA, 1961, No. 114).[23] Unfortunately, the implementation of these Ministerial Decisions was unsatisfactory as far as transmigration was concerned, very largely because transmigration was included as part of a wider programme in which the emphasis was upon development of agriculture and the introduction of land reform in Java. Despite the creation of a special Body for Co-ordination in the Implementation of Transmigration,[24] achievements in the early 1960s were no better than those in the 1950s, except for the fact that greater numbers of people were moved.

The appearance of the findings of the 1961 census, the first taken since 1930, brought home to the nation the seriousness of the population problem in Java, Madura and Bali. At various times during the first half of the 1960s, efforts were made to arouse community interest in transmigration through such programmes as the National Transmigration Movement (Statute No. 5 of 1965).[25] Quite a large number of people did in fact leave Java as a consequence of extensive government propaganda and of the participation of political parties and other non-government bodies in transmigration schemes. Attention, however, was given to numbers alone and not to the economic aspects of settling farmers in a new environment.

Meanwhile, political and economic problems took more of the government's attention. The comment made by one writer sums up the situation as it was around 1965–6:

Increasing economic difficulties have caused some disenchantment with the transmigration program, both because of its expense and because in many in-
stances the settlers leave their holdings after a few seasons and move to nearby towns or, if possible, back to Java. It would seem that the program no longer occupies an important place in government policy....[26]

Government interest in transmigration did, however, reappear and in 1967 a three-year plan was prepared to cover the period when economic stabilization was the major aim of the new government. This was ultimately replaced by a five-year plan, integrated into the First Five-Year Development Plan, wherein transmigration was given an important place in policies for regional development.

The 1967 plan had placed considerable emphasis upon the establishment of settlements in tidal areas in South Sumatra and Central and South Kalimantan.[27] But it proved impossible to carry out the original plan since preparation of the necessary water supply and drainage canals required much more time than was anticipated and the Public Works section responsible for such infrastructure could not complete the work in time. Hence a basic shift in policy again occurred when it was decided in 1969 to place most of the migrants for 1969–71 in non-tidal areas. Much more realistic and attainable targets were set for the 1969–74 period and attention was given to the economic viability of projects and not merely to the numbers of people placed in each settlement.

Achievements between 1950 and March 1969

If seen in the light of either population reduction in Java or of regional development outside Java, the results achieved by transmigration in the years immediately following independence were negligible. In the years from 1950 to 1958, 185 768 people were placed in transmigration settlements, which then covered 57 475 hectares of cultivated land. At the end of December 1958, there were 293 523 people living in these settlements; this figure includes local people living within project boundaries, independent migrants who moved into projects entirely of their own accord and children born in project areas.[28] In the years between 1959 and March 1969, another 238 612 people were moved. Less than half a million people left Java, Madura, Bali and Lombok under transmigration schemes (Table 5) during this nineteen-year period, clearly a long way from the dreams of the early 1950s, when policy-makers had talked of moving a couple of million each year.

The recruiting of migrants was the task of the branch offices set up in the capitals of the provinces of Java and in Bali, as well as in a few of the larger towns. The work of these offices was then, as it is today, to spread information among village communities in such a way that farmers and landless agricultural labourers would become interested in moving away from overcrowded areas. Another task was to select suitable migrants. Unfortunately, in the past the main criterion tended to be willingness to migrate. In some instances, notably in disaster areas where floods or volcanic eruptions had occurred, pressure was brought to bear to force homeless people to migrate. The fact that the provincial transmigration offices frequently did not give pros-

Table 6
Number of Migrants by Area of Settlement, 1950–1968

Year	Sumatra	Kalimantan	Sulawesi	Elsewhere	Total
1950	77				77
1951	2 453		96	402[1]	2 951
1952	16 585		338	682	17 605
1953	33 212	2 619	310	3 868	40 009
1954	26 430	1 736	1 078	494[2]	29 738
1955	17 609	2 033	1 314	433	21 389
1956	22 135	2 119	96		24 350
1957	17 456	4 184	1 590		23 230
1958	25 700	463		256[3]	26 419
1959	44 124	1 412	298	262	46 096
1960	19 128	2 947			22 075
1961	14 876	4 330	263	140	19 609
1962	13 966	7 543	420	200	22 129
1963	28 903	1 808	1 448		32 159
1964	11 787	2 448	987		15 222
1965	46 287	5 019	1 919		53 225
1966	771	375	2 774	728[4]	4 648
1967	7 149	652	1 015	750	9 566
1968	9 664	2 010	1 922	287	13 883

Source: 1950–1955, Directorate-General for Transmigration.
1956–1968, *Statistical Pocketbooks of Indonesia*, 1957 to 1970–1.

Notes: [1] People placed 'elsewhere' in 1951, 1952 and 1953 went to Banten, West Java (see text, p. 29).
[2] Of these people, 414 went to Maluku and 80 to Banten; the people who moved 'elsewhere' in 1955 also went to Maluku.
[3] Those placed 'elsewhere' in 1958, 1959, 1961 and 1962 were local people from Nusatenggara who were resettled in western Lombok, except for 4 persons placed in Maluku in 1958.
[4] Those placed 'elsewhere' in 1966, 1967 and 1968 went to Irian Jaya.

pective migrants a true picture of what to expect in their new homes partly explains the disappointment that many experienced and the return to Java of large numbers, particularly in the 1960s. This in turn discouraged the flow of completely independent migrants that could otherwise have been expected. The provincial offices often encouraged urban people without jobs to move to transmigration settlements, in an attempt to solve immediate employment problems in the cities of Java. Many of those who left projects shortly after arrival were non-farmers who felt that they had no hope of making a living from agriculture in the geographical conditions of the other islands.

Most of the people moved during this period came from Java. No particular policies were followed in the selection of areas from which migrants were taken. Once again, the main criterion was willingness to move. It is apparent now that if more attention had been given in the 1950s and 1960s to population reduction in densely populated areas like the Upper Solo, Serayu and Cimanuk basins, these parts of Java would perhaps be in a slightly less critical condition than they are today. Table 5 shows the area of origin of migrants moved before the beginning of the Five-Year Plan. The large number that left Bali in 1963 (70 per cent of the total for that year) is a direct reflection of the violent and completely unexpected eruption of Mt. Agung in March 1963, when thousands of hectares of terraced, irrigated rice-fields were destroyed.

From the point of view of the receiving end, that is, the provinces where the migrants were settled, many difficulties arose, a major problem being the preparation of land before the arrival of the settlers. Where projects were extensions of pre-1941 Dutch colonization settlements, preparations for newcomers did not require very much work. But where completely new projects were established on sites only partly surveyed, the problem of land clearing frequently hindered the settlement

and adjustment of migrants. In 1952 a special organization known as the *Yayasan Pembukaan Tanah* (Land-Clearing Foundation) was set up by the government to undertake large-scale clearing of tracts of land intended for transmigration purposes. The Foundation, which was government-financed, did some clearing work itself, but it also entrusted work to private contractors. Its undertakings, however, were limited to Lampung, where, between 1953 and 1958, 16 874 hectares of land were cleared in the Sukadana, Punggur and Kota Gajah areas. The Foundation was also supposed to build roads to link projects with the provincial road network; however, very little was accomplished in the field of road construction either. The Foundation was abolished in 1959 because of its rather ambiguous nature; it was financed by the government, yet it functioned like a private body in that it determined its own policies, financial and otherwise.[29] Its place was taken by the *Biro Pembukaan Tanah* (Land-Clearing Bureau), which had a clearly defined position as a section within the transmigration agency itself. Actual achievements in land clearing and road construction, however, were no better than during the 1950s.

In 1972 an official statement of the Directorate-General for Transmigration recorded a total of 124 projects (Table 7) established since 1950.[30] At the end of March 1972, only 37 of these projects had been handed over to local provincial governments, while another 23 were ready for transfer. It should be noted in any discussion of transmigration that the term 'project' has in the past been used very loosely by the transmigration authority itself. In some instances it referred to a tract of land on which several villages had been established, possibly at different times. In other cases one village of less than a hundred families was described as a project, in the sense that it was not connected with other settlements; the widely scattered and often very small settlements made in East Kalimantan, for example, were counted as separate

Table 7
Transmigration Projects by Province, 1950–March, 1972

Province	Number of projects	Area in hectares[1]	Number of migrants[2]
1. Lampung	24	252 143·5	213 332
2. Bengkulu	7	14 500	8 790
3. South Sumatra	8	57 700	82 800
4. Jambi	3	4 000	5 058
5. Riau	2	4 100	1 782
6. West Sumatra	13	44 186	17 786
7. North Sumatra	4	6 477	7 211
8. Aceh	2	22 172	1 186
SUMATRA	63	405 278·5	337 945
9. West Kalimantan	8	69 200	7 254
10. South Kalimantan	7	15 501	12 117
11. East Kalimantan	20	52 593	23 710
12. Central Kalimantan	4	7 200	7 434
KALIMANTAN	39	144 494	50 515
13. North Sulawesi	3	38 200	7 076
14. Central Sulawesi	7	43 071·5	12 416
15. South Sulawesi	3	18 538	4 767
16. South-east Sulawesi	3	2 176	2 889
SULAWESI	16	101 985·5	27 148
17. Maluku	2	1 400	1 117
18. Irian Jaya	4	–	728
TOTAL	124	653 158	417 453

Source: Compiled from data in *Laporan Tahunan Tahun ke-3, Pelita I, 1971/1972*, Departemen Transmigrasi dan Koperasi (Jakarta, 1972), Enclosure IV.

Note: [1] Area refers to total land available to projects and not to land under cultivation.
[2] Number of migrants refers to people settled in projects at various times in the 1950–72 period; it does not include those born in projects or those who moved into projects as completely independent migrants, nor does it take into account those who left projects.

projects. Sometimes extensions to existing settlements have been described as new projects (for example, Palaran in East Kalimantan), but often they have not been classed as new undertakings, an example being Belitang in South Sumatra. Although the Belitang project was officially transferred in 1962, migrants have continued to be sent to the villages in the area, which is still referred to as the Belitang project.

In past years it was customary to classify transmigration undertakings and migrants according to the organization responsible for implementation and the type of financing provided. The major category has always been General Transmigration (*Transmigrasi Umum*), which is fully sponsored and carried out by the government transmigration agency, using its own funds and facilities. General Transmigration was commenced in 1952. In

1950 and 1951 the system of Family Transmigration (*Transmigrasi Keluarga*) had been followed; the migrants who left Java were relatives of people living in Dutch colonization settlements. Since it was obvious that transmigration could not be limited to those who had connexions in project areas, General Transmigration was introduced and after January 1953 distinctions between 'general' and 'family' migrants were done away with. All migrants received the same allowances in the form of free transportation, a little pocket-money, free land already cleared, and food until the first crop was harvested. Other assistance, which involved a house already constructed, tools and seed, was to be repaid to the government; however, the fact that migrants have always found it hard to repay loans because of the slow economic progress in most settlements has made General Transmigration an expensive undertaking for the government. It should be noted that the actual assistance given to those moving under General Transmigration has varied from time to time and also from place to place. Sometimes migrants have found that the land was not cleared before they arrived, or else that only large trees had been removed; they have had to spend valuable time on clearing away bushes, undergrowth and *alang-alang* grass and have therefore been unable to plant crops for the first three or four seasons. Even then, it has usually taken several years for a family to bring its full allocation of land under cultivation. This has meant that frequently the government has been obliged to continue help in the form of basic necessities (rice, salt, salted fish, frying oil and kerosene) for much longer than the stipulated time, which was originally eight months but in recent years has been twelve months. Where crops have failed, the government has likewise had to provide foodstuffs for General Transmigrants, who have always been the full responsibility of the transmigration authority.

The second major category in the past was Special Transmigration (*Transmigrasi Khu-*

sus), which involved the movement of people for some special purpose or reason. Private Transmigration, undertaken by non-government bodies, came into this category, as did Sectoral Transmigration, in which certain sectors of government departments and bodies, as well as other organizations, were involved. The government agency most frequently concerned in Sectoral Transmigration has been the Department of Social Welfare, which has tried to help victims of natural disasters by moving them from Java and Bali; it has also sought to deal with problems of homelessness and unemployment in urban areas by settling such people, including beggars and physically handicapped people, in projects in the other islands. In some cases, provincial governments both in Java and in less populated provinces of the other islands have worked together with the transmigration authority through Sectoral Transmigration to move people. In 1954 the government resettled 1 012 people of Indonesian origin who were repatriated from Surinam in the Tongar project in West Sumatra under Special Transmigration.

The third category, Local Transmigration or *Transmigrasi Lokal* has involved the resettlement of people within the same island or, more commonly, within the same province, under government guidance. In such cases the provincial governments have usually shared in the work and provided part of the finance needed for resettlement. In the early 1950s the government felt it necessary to move people from the eastern part of the Priangan district in West Java because of security disturbances caused by the illegal activities of the Darul Islam organization. Large numbers of people had begun leaving their villages because of terrorist activities, thus adding to the already large flow of rural people seeking employment in towns and cities. The government established settlements at Cibogo, Trate and Pamengkang in Banten in the western part of the same province and 5 032 people were settled there between 1951 and 1954.[31] In the 1950s and early 1960s large numbers of people who had moved in earlier years to Lampung moved again to newer transmigration settlements and were classed as Local Transmigrants (see Table 5). In more recent years the term 'local' has been used more specifically for indigenous people who have been resettled within transmigration settlements.

The final category of Independent Transmigration (*Transmigrasi Spontan*) refers to two completely different kinds of migrants. As used by the government transmigration agency, the term indicates migrants who are helped by the government to a certain limited extent. These migrants fall into two groups: those who are described as *spontan dengan bantuan biaya* (*Spontan D.B.B.*), which means that some financial assistance is given in the form of transportation and housing materials, and those who are described as *spontan tanpa bantuan biaya* (*Spontan T.B.B.*), which means that nothing is given other than uncleared land in a transmigration project. People who move in this way, either with or without assistance but under the sponsorship of the transmigration agency, are counted in government statistics as independent or *spontan* migrants.

The term *spontan* is also used, perhaps more correctly, for independent migrants who move entirely of their own accord without the sponsorship or even the knowledge of the government transmigration agency and without any kind of assistance from the government. Since they settle where they please, renting or buying land from local people, it is impossible to know exactly how many migrate in this way each year. Over the years many of these unsponsored migrants have in fact settled in project areas; some of the discrepancies apparent in transmigration statistics can be traced to the fact that sometimes completely independent settlers have been included in annual population counts made by local officials in settlement areas.

The ultimate goal in transmigration is to set up a flow of 'spontaneous' migrants who move from overcrowded areas of their own accord and without government assistance. This has in fact been happening for many years in Lampung, where proximity to Java makes transportation relatively easy and inexpensive. In the early 1950s, more than 35 000 people from various parts of Java settled in the Way Sekampung area of Lampung, 'finding their own way and following members of their family, relatives or friends from the same place of origin, who had already preceded them to Lampung.'[32] The strength of this 'family-encouraged' pattern of migration has been underestimated by the transmigration authority in its efforts over the years to encourage people to move from Java, though it was the pattern envisaged by the Dutch colonial government when the *keluarga* system was introduced into the colonization programme in 1937.

If, however, people are to become interested in joining relatives and friends in new settlements, those settlements must offer definite possibilities for a better life. It has sometimes been concluded that the Javanese farmer is unwilling to leave his home village. Experiences in transmigration since 1950 have shown that this is not so, if other regions offer hopes for a higher standard of living. Similarly, the spontaneous movement of Balinese to Sulawesi in the years since the eruption of Mt. Agung indicates a willingness to migrate among the people of this tiny island. It is essential, however, that there be positive attractions, the 'push-factor', encouraging people to migrate,

... cannot simply be equated with the degree of poverty among the rural unemployed in overcrowded regions. It cannot be taken for granted that there is an automatic correlation between poverty and the desire to migrate.[33]

Most of the facilities necessary to attract more unsponsored migrants are precisely those needed for regional development, such as good roads, adequate means of transportation, regular water supplies and the like. In a situation where independent migration was taking place on a large scale, the role of the transmigration authority itself would be reduced to the selection of suitable settlement sites, the handling of any legal claims to the land by other parties and the giving of guidance in agricultural methods and cropping patterns. All concerned would benefit from the 'capital' that the completely independent migrant brings with him in the form of initiative and enterprise.

Transmigration during the First Five-Year Plan

The First Five-Year Development Plan, which began in April 1969, in an attempt to re-invigorate the Indonesian economy after the economic and political troubles of the 1960s, focused attention on both agricultural expansion and regional development as being essential for overall national development. Agricultural development, as described in the Plan, has involved an intensification of existing farming methods (primarily in Java), diversification of cropping patterns (in Java and in other islands also) and the opening up of new

agricultural land (in the islands other than Java and Bali).[34] It is to the third of these aspects that transmigration is relevant. The Plan placed transmigration in the wider perspective of regional development:

In the context of the implementation of the Five-Year Development Plan, transmigration is linked with developmental undertakings and activities and does not stand alone. Thus transmigration undertakings are to provide support for developmental undertakings in the provinces and for projects that require labour.[35]

During the 1969–74 period, a constant effort was made to integrate transmigration plans into more general plans for the development of the natural resources in each province. Transmigration is now seen more as a land-development programme in areas outside Java rather than as a means of reducing population pressure in Java.

At the beginning of the First Five-Year Plan, the whole mechanism of the transmigration agency, changed in status to a Directorate-General in 1968, was in such a disorganized condition that only relatively small

Table 8

Number of Migrants by Area of Origin, 1969–1974

Area of origin	1969–70	1970–1	1971–2	1972–3	1973–4	Total
West Java	2 105	3 004	2 647	7 936	8 170[1]	23 862
Central Java	4 093	5 979	4 119	15 455	27 778	57 424
Special Area of Yogyakarta	5 397	2 636	2 739	5 916	6 212	22 900
East Java	4 726	3 475	4 139	16 850	24 966	54 156
Bali	1 527	4 901	5 226	5 761	4 380	21 795
Lombok					1 451	1 451
Local[2]					108	108
	17 848	19 995	18 870	51 918	73 065	181 696

Source: Directorate-General for Transmigration, Jakarta.

Notes: [1]The 1973–74 figure for West Java includes 1 433 people from the Capital Territory of Jakarta.

[2]'Local' refers to indigenous people moving into project areas.

numbers of people could be moved in 1969, 1970 and 1971. Table 8 gives details of the number of migrants leaving Java, Bali and Lombok in the years between 1969 and 1974. More than half of these people went to Sumatra where, in most cases, they were settled in existing projects (Table 9).

As was pointed out above, the policies drawn up in the years immediately preceding the beginning of the Five-Year Plan had involved the settlement of large numbers of migrants in tidal areas. But since it proved impossible to prepare the necessary water channels for tidal irrigation, a change in plans was made:

... thus with the approval of the President, and in co-ordination with *Bappenas*, a specific policy was formulated. The basis of this policy involved further 'switching' of the targets for tidal areas and the formulation of a Crash Program.[36]

The Crash Program referred to involved the selection of other sites where land could be obtained immediately. The migrants who should have gone to tidal projects were settled in dry-farming districts in Lampung, South Sumatra, Riau and South Sulawesi. However, as a consequence of inadequate survey work, hurried planning and insufficient preparation, not all of these projects have prospered.

During the first two years of the Five-Year Plan, the emphasis was of necessity upon rehabilitation work. Many of the settlements established in the first half of the 1960s had not progressed from the economic point of view, since virtually no attention was given to them once the migrants had reached the project sites. Rehabilitation work covered many different aspects, from the provision of foodstuffs to the construction of urgently needed roads and bridges.

In some instances rehabilitation has meant resettlement of migrants who had been placed in badly selected locations that offered no hope for real development. Sometimes resettlement has been necessary for other reasons, a good example being the Gunung Balak settlers in Central Lampung. The original settlements in this area were made in the early 1960s by organizations outside the competence of the transmigration authority.[37] The settlements, however, were within a reserved forest zone. In 1972 the Directorate-General for Transmigration was given the task of shifting migrants from the area. Most were reluctant to move since the soil of Gunung Balak is fertile and crops were doing well. They have been resettled in the Way Abung and Panaragan projects, 534 families (2 075 people) going to the village of Bumirestu in the former project in 1972–3 and another 75 families (205 people) going to the village of Candraken-

Table 9
Number of Migrants by Area of Settlement, 1969–1974

Area of settlement	1969–70	1970–1	1971–2	1972–3	1973–4	Total
Sumatra	11 112	8 350	9 002	31 783	44 977	105 224
Kalimantan	2 599	3 970	4 748	7 227	8 038	26 582
Sulawesi	4 137	7 442	5 120	11 944	19 049	47 692
Maluku		233		479	1 001	1 713
Irian Jaya				485		485
	17 848	19 995	18 870	51 918	73 065	181 696

Source: Directorate-General for Transmigration, Jakarta.

cana in the latter project in 1973–4, together with 108 local indigenous people.

One further aspect of resettlement work has been the planned movement of indigenous people into transmigration project areas, the purpose being to help local people to benefit from project facilities and thus to improve their own economic position. This has been of particular significance in areas where forests are being destroyed by shifting cultivators. In East Kalimantan the provincial government has made attempts of its own to resettle shifting cultivators in areas of permanent cultivation. It has proved more effective to combine such efforts with transmigration projects, since migrants from Java and Bali already have traditions of sedentary agriculture and from the financial point of view, it is preferable to establish larger projects to accommodate both groups of people. This policy has the further advantage of preventing the transmigration projects from becoming Javanese or Balinese enclaves and of encouraging assimilation at an early stage.

As a result of the attention given to rehabilitation work and to the surveying of new sites in 1969, 1970 and 1971, it was possible to move a far greater number of migrants in 1972–3, when the number shifted (51 918 people) was almost equal to the number moved in the preceding three-year period. As Table 8 shows, the number moved in the fifth year of the Five-Year Plan was much greater (73 065 people). The emphasis, however, has been not on the numbers of migrants but on the establishment of a satisfactory economic foundation that will enable each project to develop with its own resources.

During the First Five-Year Plan, 181 696 people (39 727 families) were settled in transmigration projects. Most of these people migrated from Java, Madura, Bali and Lombok, but some were local people who were resettled or who moved of their own accord into project areas. Of those who moved, 37 165 people (7 930 families) went to tidal projects in eastern Sumatra and southern and western Kali-

mantan. During this period the Directorate-General for Transmigration was responsible for migrants living in projects established before 1969 but not yet transferred to the local government in the provinces concerned. A major obstacle to transfer has been agrarian problems, which have continued to exist because of inadequate attention in early years to the status of project land and to the surveying of holdings allocated to migrants. In some cases, the lack of economic growth has delayed transfer to the ordinary governmental administration system. Allowances have been made in the 1974–5 budget of the Directorate-General to provide money for the settlement of land status problems through the correct legal channels, the registration of holdings given to each migrant family and the granting of land-ownership certificates. The older projects are to be transferred during 1974–5. Steps will also be taken to make possible the transfer of the 1969–70 projects during 1975–6, in accordance with the policy stated in the Basic Transmigration Act of 1972 of a five-year period of guidance before the provincial government takes over responsibility for the settlements.

During this period there was an increase in the number of people migrating to project areas with very little or no assistance from the government agency. In the 1969–74 period, 54 645 people (12 259 families) out of the total number of migrants moved under the *spontan* programme. Some received financial assistance while others received only uncleared land. Shortly before the end of the 1973–4 financial year, a new programme, *Transmigrasi Spontan Bantuan Presiden*, known as the *Banpres* programme, was commenced to encourage greater numbers of partly assisted migrants to leave Java and Bali. Special Presidential funds were provided to cover transportation and basic necessities for four months for 6 000 families. By the beginning of June 1974, 3 693 families (16 269 people) had moved under this programme, settling in most cases in projects still under the care of the transmigration agency. Those who settled in older projects already transferred to the local government will receive guidance in agricultural methods from the local Transmigration Directorate until they are properly established in their new homes. In some cases these migrants have been helped by the *Yayasan Makarti Mukti Tama*, a foundation intended to be: 'the arm of the Transmigration Agency in mobilising community participation'.[38] The foundation is non-commercial in nature; its main function so far has been to arouse interest in migration among farmers who are not completely without money and who have enough initiative to want to better themselves, and to help partly assisted migrants to settle in project areas.

During the First Five-Year Plan it was the policy of the Directorate-General for Transmigration to send partly assisted migrants to well-established projects like Belitang in South Sumatra and Parigi in Central Sulawesi. Those people moving under General Transmigration, since they received much more help in the form of houses and basic necessities, as well as seed, tools and clothes, were usually placed in new projects, where heavier work is required in the early stages. As from 1974, however, distinctions will no longer be made between *umum* and *spontan* migrants.

When the Second Five-Year Plan was commenced in April 1974, there were 61 projects officially under guidance, with eight new ones ready for settlement in the second half of 1974. This number does not include untransferred projects established before 1969–70, but it does take in Department of Social Welfare projects established for natural-disaster victims and handed over to the transmigration agency for guidance and supervision. The 61 projects consisted of 103 village units, with 17 village units planned for the 8 new projects. Present policies, first introduced in 1973, require that a project should consist of approximately 10 village units so as to achieve greater impact upon the economic expansion of the surrounding area. Thus it will no longer happen that a village of a few hundred people will be classed as a project.

A significant step forward was taken in 1972 with the ratification of the Basic Transmigration Act, which has provided basic legislation for the expansion of the transmigration programme. Many of the obstacles that hindered the successful implementation of transmigration in the first twenty years after independence have been removed and a firmer basis has been laid for the development of settlements in coming years. That transmigration will continue to be a major national policy is made quite clear in the Second Five-Year Development Plan, which will guide national development during the 1974–9 period.

[1] For a discussion of the Ethical Policy, see B.H.M. Vlekke, *Nusantara*, rev. ed. (Bruxelles and Jakarta, 1961), pp. 331-3, and J.D. Legge, *Indonesia*, Prentice-Hall, Inc. (New Jersey, 1964), pp. 86-95.

[2] Anwas Adiwilaga, 'Pembahasan peranan dan pengaruh Transmigrasi dalam pembinaan persatuan dan kesatuan Bangsa' (Discussion of the role and influence of Transmigration in the fostering of National union and unity) in *Arti dan Peranan Transmigrasi di Indonesia*, P.T. Makarti Djaya (Jakarta, 1970), p. 96.

[3] M. Amral Sjamsu, *Dari Kolonisasi ke Transmigrasi*, Djambatan (Jakarta, 1960), p. 5.

[4] In a footnote concerning the Coolie Ordinance of 1880, which referred to labour recruitment for north-eastern Sumatra, J.D. Legge points out that 'its main purpose, reflected in the penal sanction that was applied to laborers who neglected their work or deserted, was to give the employer almost complete control of the laborer'. Legge, op. cit., p. 83.

[5] In fact, no colonization settlements were established in North Sumatra, due to differences of opinion between the provincial government and the central government about methods to be employed. The plantations continued to recruit their own labour as before, and in many cases established their own 'colonies', in some instances in co-operation with the local provincial government.

[6] Amral Sjamsu, op. cit., pp. 38-9 (1/10 is common nowadays in Java).

[7] The word *Way* means River.

[8] Amral Sjamsu, op. cit., p. 108.

[9] The remainder came from other parts of Sumatra. Amral Sjamsu, op. cit., p. 18.

[10] Fisher, op. cit., p. 294.

[11] The local resident was given authority to control expansion in the capacity of the mills and to ensure that the mills did not purchase too much rice from farmers. Amral Sjamsu, op. cit., pp. 15-16.

[12] The word *marga*, as used in southern Sumatra, refers to an area of land occupied by a group of people under traditional law.

[13] R. Soebiantoro, *Transmigration and the Prospects It Offers for Prosperity and Security*, Department of Transmigration and Co-operatives (Jakarta, 1971), p. 25.

[14] The Japanese made an attempt to shift people to the Batanghari Utara area in Lampung, which had already been surveyed by the Dutch; 1 867 families from Java and 355 families from Bangka were placed there but results were unsatisfactory since most of the people moved were not farmers. After independence the name of the settlement was changed to Purbolinggo. Amral Sjamsu, op. cit., p. 77.

[15] Although independence was proclaimed on 17 August 1945, sovereignty was recognized only on 27 December 1949, after four years of heavy fighting.

[16] Mohammad Hatta, 'Pokok-Pokok Sambutan' (Main Points of Addresses of Welcome), No. 2, in *Arti dan Peranan Transmigrasi di Indonesia*, P.T. Makarti Djaya (Jakarta, 1970), pp. 181-2.

[17] This Decree referred to the return to the 1945 Constitution; it marked the commencement of Guided Democracy.

[18] Amral Sjamsu, op. cit., p. 81.

[19] *Garis-Garis Besar Rentjana Pembangunan Lima Tahun 1956-60*, State Planning Bureau (Jakarta, 1956), p. 258.

[20] *Rantjangan Dasar Undang-Undang Pembangunan Nasional-Semesta-Berentjana Delapan Tahun: 1961-1969*, National Planning Board (Jakarta, 1960), Vol. XII, p. 2467.

[21] Ibid., pp. 2537-8.

[22] Ibid., p. 2597.

[23] *Pola Kerdja Sama Departemen Transkopemada dengan Departemen-Departemen Lain*, Department of Transmigration, Co-operatives and Rural Community Development (Jakarta (no date)), pp. 22, 29 and 33.

[24] *Rantjangan Dasar Undang-Undang Pembangunan Nasional-Semesta-Berentjana Delapan Tahun: 1961-9*, op. cit., p. 2536.

[25] This Statute and Statute No. 29 of 1960 concerning the Basis for Implementation of Transmigration were revoked in the Basic Transmigration Act of 1972.

[26] G. McNicoll, 'Internal Migration in Indonesia: Descriptive Notes', in *Indonesia*, No. 5 April 1968, p. 69.

[27] *Perumusan Hasil-Hasil Rapat Kerdja Transmigrasi*, 24-7 February 1969, Solo.

[28] *Rantjangan Dasar Undang-Undang Pembangunan Nasional-Semesta-Berentjana Delapan Tahun: 1961-1969*, op. cit., pp. 2543-50.

[29] Soedigdo Hardjosudarmo, *Kebidjaksanaan Transmigrasi Dalam Rangka Pembangunan Masjarakat Desa di Indonesia*, Bhratara (Jakarta, 1965), pp. 154-6.

[30] *Laporan Tahunan, Tahun ke-3, Pelita I, 1971/72*, Directorate-General for Transmigration (Jakarta, 1972), Enclosure IV.

[31] Soedigdo Hardjosudarmo has pointed out that these three projects, intended as permanent settlements, were deserted in the early 1960s, the people having returned of their own accord to their villages of origin in the much more fertile Priangan district after the collapse of the Darul Islam movement in 1962 (Soedigdo Hardjosudarmo, op. cit., pp. 167-8).

[32] Kampto Utomo, 'Masjarakat Transmigran Spontan Didaerah W. Sekampung (Lampung)' in *Tehnik Pertanian*, July-Sept. 1958, p. 327.

[33] R. Soebiantoro, *Transmigration and the Prospects It Offers for Prosperity and Security*, op. cit., p. 17.

[34] *Rentjana Pembangunan Lima Tahun 1969/70-1973/74*, Department of Information (Jakarta, 1968), I, pp. 15-23.

[35] Ibid., II C, pp. 109-10.

[36] *Laporan Kegiatan Tahun I Pelita 1969-1970*, Department of Transmigration and Co-operatives (Jakarta, 1970), p. 9. (*Bappenas* is the National Planning Board.)

[37] *Laporan Tahunan Tahun ke-3, Pelita I, 1971/72*, Directorate-General for Transmigration (Jakarta, 1972), p. 6.

[38] *Petunjuk Umum Pelaksanaan Untuk Program Kerja Transmigrasi 1973/1974 Dalam Menyongsong Repelita II*, Directorate-General for Transmigration (Jakarta, 1973), p. 15.

IV
Past Problems

Attitudes to Transmigration

A fundamental problem in past years, if it can be called a problem rather than an underlying misconception about the whole idea of transmigration, lay in the attitudes taken towards government-sponsored schemes. During the 1950s and most of the 1960s transmigration was seen almost entirely in demographic terms. Despite vague government statements about improvements in living standards among rural communities, the shifting of people from overcrowded areas was seen as a means of solving Java's population problems by both government and people alike. Many, however, regarded transmigration as a waste of money, for it was obviously making no impression upon population density, and could hardly be expected to do so, with a population growth of well over 2 per cent a year. It was felt, in certain government and community circles, that the money used for transmigration could be spent more effectively on agricultural intensification in Java, industrialization and general improvement of the infrastructure in all parts of the country. Indeed, transmigration projects often did consume large sums of money for which very little could be seen. On the whole, an attitude of indifference was characteristic of all concerned directly or indirectly with transmigration. Government departments often resented having to include in their budgets expenditure for roads, bridges and other facilities intended specifically for transmigration settlements. This attitude arose from inadequate definition of the financial responsibilities of the transmigration authority itself, but it reflected the general attitude that transmigration was not really an essential undertaking.

Attitudes of this kind could not be expected to encourage the necessary enthusiasm among migrants themselves, as one writer has pointed out in speaking of transmigration in the 1950s:

> The Government's attitude in transmigration undertakings at that time could be described as paternalistic. This clearly did not have good results. Within the transmigration communities there arose an attitude of dependence upon the Government for aid and subsidies. Initiative, creativity, willingness to work and dedication wilted.[1]

At the village level confused attitudes to transmigration were apparent. In the districts from which the migrants came there was a tendency to regard those who decided to migrate as the 'failures' in the community. Too often those who agreed to be moved were the less enterprising and less resourceful people in the village. Those who possessed initiative but felt that opportunities for making a good living were limited in their village moved to the urban centres of Java and not to uncultivated land in Sumatra. Usually transmigration officials simply took those people willing to move, giving little thought to their suitability. One of the consequences was that the new settlements frequently lacked leaders among the settlers themselves. Migrants tended to look upon the officials of the government transmigration authority as being responsible for every aspect of their lives after they had been settled on their holdings.

Likewise, certain attitudes in the provinces that accepted migrants were not always satisfactory. In many cases the newcomers were not well received by the local people of the area, just as had happened in the days of Dutch colonization. This attitude is to a certain extent understandable if the situation is examined in more detail, for there were many very fundamental faults inherent in the way in which transmigration programmes were carried out in the past.

In most cases there was insufficient consultation between the transmigration authority and the local provincial government about the actual implementation of settlement work. Local authorities often felt that they were by-passed by transmigration officials, who tended to overlook the fact that settlements would in the long run have to become part of the provincial administrative structure. At the same time, preparations for the settlement of migrants were usually inadequate. The accusation made by provincial authorities that transmigration meant 'the transfer of rural poverty' was indeed justified in more than one case. The new settlers sometimes became a burden upon existing local communities, which were in no position to support more individuals without an accompanying input of facilities like roads and water supplies.

A further reason for the disfavour in which many people at all levels of the community held transmigration in the past can be traced to the political motives involved in some, though certainly not all, settlements. In the mid-1950s the government was faced with the problem of the Darul Islam disturbances, referred to in the preceding chapter. Settlements were established in Banten for village people who had been forced to leave their fields. Many villagers, however, were detained on charges of assisting those responsible for the disturbances or of actually being members of rebel bands. It was decided (Presidential Decree No. 54 of 1954) to give the Transmigration Service the task of resettling such people some distance from their homes in West Java. In 1954, 841 families (1 950 persons) were moved in this way, while another 326 families (1 052 persons) were shifted in 1955.[2] Naturally, such people were not eager to move, nor is it surprising that they were not well received in the areas where they were settled.

More serious was a later development in the early 1960s, when certain political parties, notably the now banned Indonesian Communist Party, made use of transmigration for their own political ends. Admittedly, the government of the period was very much responsible for what happened, for in the years immediately before 1965 it had followed a policy 'of encouraging large-scale transmigration and of letting community organizations (Ormas) participate in the implementation of transmigration'.[3] The community organizations referred to were affiliated with the various political parties of the time. There was, however, no control over such transfers of people; indeed, in the political conditions then existing, any supervision by the government transmigration authority was a virtual impossibility. The result of haphazard undertakings, intended by a political party for the purpose of obtaining influence in certain areas, was the establishment of badly planned settlements in which no thought was given to soil conditions, availability of water or land rights, let alone to the attitudes of the local residents. The very large number of people moved in 1965 (53 225—the largest in any year between 1950 and 1973) was the result of such politically motivated transmigration schemes.

A further reason for the resentment shown towards transmigration by the indigenous people of settlement areas lay in the fact that the Department of Social Welfare had attempted to solve some of its own problems by settling homeless, unemployed people from urban districts in Java on agricultural land in other parts of Indonesia. These projects failed in most cases, usually because the settlers concerned had no interest at all in farming and in fact tended to abandon their holdings and move to cities and towns, where they proved a burden to local authorities. The transmigration authority itself had had the same experience when non-farmers were moved to new rural settlements.

Associated with the demographic approach to transmigration, though founded on different motives, was the attitude that transmigration should 'fill the empty spaces' in the interests of national defence and security. This attitude, though not stressed so much today, has not disappeared and Clause 2 of the 1972 Transmigration Act makes specific mention of the defence-security aspect of transmigration when it states that the seventh and last aim in transmigration is 'a strengthening of national defence and security'. However, it is now generally recognized that such considerations must not be allowed to take priority over economic aspects in the selection of sites for settlements.

Authority for Implementation

In the past lack of interdepartmental co-ordination not just in transmigration but in regional development also gave rise to many difficulties in the implementation of transmigration policies and programmes. A major reason for this lack of co-ordination lay in the fact that the competence of the government body entrusted with transmigration matters was never properly defined. Thus it often happened that settlements were made in areas without adequate water supplies in the expectation that the Department of Public Works would construct the necessary irrigation facilities. Often, however, Public Works had no such plans or, if plans had existed, they had not been carried out because of a shift in priorities occasioned by other factors that were often of a political nature.

The Way Seputih project illustrates this lack of co-ordination. In the Five-Year Plan for 1956–1960 it was stated that a new irrigation project would be commenced by the Public Works Department in the Way Seputih area.[4] Nothing was done until 1968, however. The consequences for the transmigration villages established in the area are discussed in the next chapter. Another more recent example is the case of the plan to settle large numbers of migrants in tidal areas in the late 1960s. The fact that the Public Works Department could not prepare the necessary canal networks in time resulted in the policy change already described above. Once again, the lack of co-

ordination between departments in the original preparation of plans led to difficulties in implementation. Authority for implementation was supposed to lie with the transmigration agency but inadequate co-ordination proved a constant handicap.

A further complication arose in cases where more than one body had authority in matters relating to the movement of people. A good example is the case of natural disasters, where the Department of Social Welfare itself moved disaster victims to areas outside Java and Bali. After the eruption of Mt. Agung in Bali in 1963, 22 958 people were moved from southeastern Bali, some of them by the Department of Social Welfare and the rest by the transmigration agency. Thus there was often duplication of activities; the fact that the Department of Social Welfare was not equipped for pre-settlement survey work nor capable of giving guidance to new settlers in agriculture, marketing and community development meant that many new villages did not prosper.

The major problem that has arisen when bodies other than the government transmigration authority moved migrants has been one of responsibility. It often happened in the past that the organization concerned did not see the task through. In the case of the politically inspired projects of the mid-1960s, no further attention was given to the migrants once they had reached the project area. Often finance was the problem, for there was insufficient input of the items needed to help the new villages to develop. The migrants then turned to the government for assistance, feeling that the government should bear all the responsibility. The transmigration authority, however, had enough to do in handling its own mistakes and could usually give very little assistance to the 'victims' of privately organized schemes.

With the ratification of the Basic Transmigration Act of 1972 and the follow-up Regulation for the Implementation of Transmigration (No. 42 of 1973), authority for all transmigration has been placed in the hands of one minister, namely the Minister for Manpower, Transmigration and Co-operatives, in an attempt to prevent the movement of people by organizations, both government and private, that do not have the funds and resources necessary for successful settlement of migrants. Government bodies require the Minister's approval for any proposed undertakings, while non-government organizations require his written permission. Related to this is the expectation that there will be better co-ordination in planning and implementation and better protection for the migrant if all transmigration is the responsibility of one minister.

Land Problems

Perhaps the most serious problems in the years before 1969 were those associated with land. Field officers who have been closely involved in actual settlement work almost invariably point to land issues as the greatest hindrances to the successful establishment of projects. Four basic, inter-related problems are involved: the procurement of suitable sites for settlement, the handling of claims to land already selected for settlement, the size of the holding to be given to migrants and the granting of land titles after migrants have been settled.

The first of these problems has already been touched upon in what was said above about attitudes to transmigration. Provincial governments tended to feel that they had enough to do without worrying about transmigration settlements or suitable locations for them. Too often the attitude in this matter of site selection was one of 'beggars can't be choosers' and naturally local governments were reluctant to risk disturbances in their provinces over a task that was not treated as a matter of national importance. This attitude was a direct consequence of the fact that transmigration programmes were in no way integrated into provincial-level plans for regional development or local land utilization.

In the selection of project sites, insufficient attention was given to survey work. There was a lack of detailed information about the nature of soils and the availability of water throughout the year. No real thought was given to the type of crops suited to the soil and water conditions of each different district. Transmigration officials simply accepted whatever land was made available.

The second major problem involved the establishment of settlements on land that was not entirely free from prior claims. Only too often it happened that, when migrants had finally succeeded in cultivating the land allotted to them, some individual or group would appear with claims that were indisputable. One element of the shifting cultivation system has been the development of *marga* groups having hereditary rights to large, unmapped tracts of land. Legal records of such rights and of the precise boundaries of *marga* land have not existed, although the Dutch colonial government had attempted to clarify the situation in southern Sumatra.

Connected with claims to land was the problem of crops already growing on the land. It is common for shifting cultivators to plant young rubber trees on the fields they have cleared before abandoning them. The trees are left to grow without care but after some six or seven years the original cultivator returns to tap the rubber. If in the meantime migrants have been settled on the land and have either felled the trees or tapped them, a dispute occurs.[5] In some cases shifting cultivators have deliberately waited until the land was cleared again by migrants and brought under cultivation, and then presented their claims, either communally or individually, to it.[6]

The basic mistake lay with the transmigration authority itself, for not enough attention was given to ascertaining whether or not there were claims to a site that had been selected. Where claims were known to exist, they were often ignored in the hope that they would be forgotten. In other cases the authority depended upon 'influence' or upon later negotiations to settle the matter. It must also be admitted that in the past the government was often reluctant to pay just compensation to shifting cultivators or to others who had prior rights to the land. In many instances financial compensation was promised but never given, with the result that those who felt themselves deceived retaliated against the migrants. However, it should also be pointed out that those with claims sometimes demanded exorbitant sums as compensation in the belief that the government could and should pay anything to obtain land. Others held on to land in the expectation that roads and bridges would be constructed, just as land speculators do in the more sophisticated world of the cities.

The reason for these land problems can be traced to the fact that the procedure for obtaining land for transmigration projects was never very clear. Inadequate co-ordination with the government body in charge of agrarian affairs (another body that, like the transmigration authority, has been moved from one ministry to another over the years) meant that it was not always easy to have legal details about land rights settled quickly. An attempt had been made in 1961 through a Joint Ministerial Decision (No. SK 404/KA, 1961, No. 114) to place responsibility for decisions about land status upon the Department of Agrarian Affairs. The Ministerial Decision stated that:

In an accurate manner the Department of Agrarian Affairs can indicate certain lands to become transmigration projects. Thus officials of the Department of Transmigration, Co-operatives and Community Development involved in development of transmigration projects need no longer face difficulties with local indigenous people about land problems.[7]

Unfortunately, this Ministerial Decision had no effect upon actual implementation of transmigration, so far as the problem of obtaining land and avoiding land disputes was concerned. Subsequent legislation has stressed that land must be free from other claims before settlement of migrants is commenced.

Since 1972 there has been an improvement in the handling of land matters, largely as a consequence of Clause 11 (paragraph 2) of the Basic Transmigration Act, which gives the minister responsible for agrarian affairs the task of ensuring that land intended for a project is freed from all claims before it is handed over to the minister responsible for transmigration.

This issue of claims to land has a further aspect in that since 1968 the government has granted extensive forestry concessions to domestic and foreign logging companies on a basis of the 1967 Basic Forestry Act. It frequently happens that, when a relatively unpopulated area has been selected for a transmigration project, further investigation shows that it lies within a forestry concession area. So far no co-ordinated plan of action has been worked out between the transmigration and the forestry agencies, although proposals were made as long ago as 1966 for the establishment of settlements in conjunction with timber felling.[8] Unfortunately, the Basic Forestry Act, formulated at a time when national interest in transmigration had waned, gives scant attention to the land requirements of transmigration; although the Clarification to the Act (No. 2823 of 1967) emphasizes that the rights of traditional-law communities may not be allowed to stand in the way of the establishment of transmigration settlements (Clause 17), it overlooks the fact that forestry concessions might.

From the migrant's point of view the whole land issue has other aspects. Migrants have always been promised land of their own, this being one of the attractions held out to landless agricultural labourers in Java and Bali. Yet in the past stipulations were never clear about the amount of land the individual migrant would receive and the time when he should obtain full ownership rights. The general principle was that each migrant family (averaging five persons) was entitled to 2 hectares of land for a home lot and for general farming purposes, though in fact migrants in some projects received less than 2 hectares.

In providing only 2 hectares of land for each migrant family, the transmigration authority in the 1950s and 1960s was keeping fairly close to the former Dutch colonization concept of establishing new settlements on the pattern of wet-rice cultivation found in Java and Bali. It is not surprising that although the Indonesian authority has allowed 2 hectares rather than the 1 hectare given by the colonization authority, many of the same consequences have followed. Where irrigation was available, outwardly prosperous settlements developed; soon, however, overcrowding appeared as a result of natural increase and the flow into the area of completely independent migrants. Where irrigation was not provided, migrants were forced to use their 2 hectares for the cultivation of dry rice, corn and, most commonly, cassava. The transmigrant farmer has never been in a position to advance to the level of a smallholder growing cash crops, except in a few districts. The need for a larger farm allocation, at least in dry-farming areas, was realized by field officers several years ago and the suggestion was made that 3 to 5 hectares be allowed for one family;[9] however it was only considered seriously in the years after 1970.

The fourth problem connected with land is that of the granting of ownership rights to migrants. For the most part very little was done in the majority of settlements to ensure that the individual migrant received a legal title to the land he was cultivating. Resentment frequently arose among migrants towards government officials because of delays, but often the excuse given by officials was true—that the land was not yet free from the original claims. The basic problem lay in the fact that it was not within the competence of the transmigration authority to issue land deeds, a task that has always been the responsibility of the agency for agrarian affairs. Although it was stated in the early part of the 1960s that: 'Transmigrants who have already been settled for at least three years in a transmigration project are to be given ownership rights to the land they have occupied and cultivated, in keeping with the stipulations of the Basic Agrarian Act',[10] virtually nothing was done about implementation. If the transmigration authority itself had given at least land use certificates, the transfer of projects to the local provincial administration could have been greatly facilitated. In 1974 the Directorate-General for Transmigration was still trying to settle problems of land ownership within projects established in the years before 1969, with the help of Joint Decision No. 91/1973 (77/KPTS/MEN/1973) of the Ministers for Home Affairs and Manpower, Transmigration and Co-operatives, which contains stipulations for the giving of land-ownership certificates.

Status of Transmigration Projects

The actual status of projects in the past also presented problems. In many cases local provincial governments completely ignored the transmigration settlements in their provinces, while in others regional authorities tried to exert influence over them in matters like taxation at a very early stage.

Past experiences have shown that rates of growth vary considerably in the settlements, though on the whole there has been some correlation between soil fertility, water supplies and availability of markets on the one hand and economic growth on the other. The question arises: how long is the transmigration authority to be responsible for each settlement? If the Directorate-General for Transmigration has to keep putting money into projects indefinitely, the financial burden becomes so heavy that only a limited number of new projects can be established each year. In the original concept of transmigration in the 1950s, it was anticipated that it would be sufficient to settle migrants on the land, to provide seed, and to give a food allowance for the first few months until the first crop could be harvested. Facts proved that this approach was unrealistic, for local geographical conditions were not taken into account. In many instances the land was not cleared before migrants arrived. Even in cases where it was, the first crops were often disappointing because of poor soil, inadequate water and bad quality seed. The consequence was that the transmigration authority found itself spending much of its annual budget on the provision of food for migrants already settled in new villages. Quite obviously, such projects could not be transferred to the local provincial administration since they were still a long way from being self-supporting. The assumption was that a project was ready for transfer when it was 'self-supporting'. Until then, it retained its status as a transmigration project.

Table 11, which gives details of transmigration projects in Lampung between 1952 and 1973, shows the length of time that elapsed before transfer to the provincial government. In an attempt to re-organize transmigration programmes, the Directorate-General for Transmigration transferred several of the older projects at the beginning of the First Five-Year Plan, irrespective of their level of economic development.

In the interests of encouraging settlements to become self-supporting as rapidly as possible, it has been felt necessary to stipulate a certain length of time during which a project is under the care of the transmigration authority. Five years is considered to be an adequate period, assuming that there is sufficient input of the necessary facilities for economic growth when the settlement is first established. Clause 15 of the Basic Transmigration Act states that a settlement has project status for five years from the time of settlement. In an attempt to solve the problem of older projects, Government Regulation No. 42 of 1973 stipulated that any settlement established before 28 July 1967 had lost its status as a transmigration project; in the case of a project established between this date and July 1972, a report should be given on progress and permission requested to continue development of the project concerned. During the First Five-Year Development Plan, with the introduction of a special allowance from the Central Government for village development, these older settlements have found that it is in their interests to have ordinary village rather than project status as soon as possible.

Assimilation in Transmigration Areas

In any movement of people from one place to another, even within the same country, problems of assimilation inevitably arise. Problems of adjustment have appeared in transmigration projects for, apart from differences in farming patterns, there have also been differences in language and customs. Despite the fact that the significance of transmigration for national unity has always been stressed, relatively little attention has been given to encouraging assimilation between newcomers and local people.

This, along with other problems in transmigration undertakings, can be traced back to the fact that in past years transmigration was not integrated into plans for regional development. Many of the early projects were really extensions of former colonization settlements and so the enclave pattern was continued. Even where completely new projects were established, they tended to be set apart from local villages, while the occurrence of disputes over land led to greater alienation between migrants and local people.

One important though less explicitly stated expectation in transmigration programmes has been that migrants from Java and Bali would bring with them the skills associated with sedentary agriculture and thus introduce new farming patterns in areas of shifting cultivation. The mistake, however, has been to try to establish wet-rice cultivation as the only form of sedentary agriculture in project areas where in most cases the land does not have the potential for irrigated rice. On the whole, shifting cultivators have learned little from the new settlers. In fact, the departure of migrants from some of the less successful projects has been more in keeping with the farming pattern of shifting cultivators, for these settlers found that soil fertility was rapidly exhausted by the cultivation of cassava over a period of eight years or so.

Lack of assimilation in the past has given rise to feelings of resentment on the part of both local people and migrants. This was pointed out some years ago by one writer who, in speaking of the 'resocialization process' involved in the establishment of new villages, said that indigenous people in southern Lampung spoke of Javanese settlers 'in a scornful tone'.[11] That the issue is still an important one was made clear in the comments of university students from outside Java during the Seminar on Problems of Transmigration and Urbanization held at the Islamic University of Indonesia, Yogyakarta, in November 1972.[12] The question was asked why Javanese cultural values should be maintained in transmigration settlements like those in Lampung. It is interesting to note that as settlements begin to prosper economically, migrants tend to revert very noticeably to their former traditions in festivals, celebrations and religious practices.[13]

The problem of how to integrate migrants into local communities, avoiding the enclave pattern favoured by the Dutch government and in many cases unintentionally followed by the transmigration authority in the 1950s and early 1960s, but at the same time making adjustment of migrants to the new environment as easy as possible, has no ready solution. The ultimate goal for all concerned is to attain a better standard of living without either group of people having to sacrifice its cultural values. Undoubtedly, rapid solutions to any problems connected with land would lead to the better assimilation of newcomers. This could be achieved with better integration of transmigration programmes into regional development plans, and further expansion of the concept of transmigration as a land settlement programme designed for the benefit of both newcomers and local people. Definite steps have been taken since 1969 to see that local residents can enjoy facilities provided for migrants and Clause 13 of the 1972 Transmigration Act states that: 'The local inhabitants are given the opportunity to move voluntarily to the Transmigration Area and in principle they are treated as transmigrants'. Indigenous people can readily obtain any advantages offered to transmigrants (such as land, food supplies and seed) but they are likewise obliged to observe all regulations binding upon the newcomers. The number of local people moving into project areas has been increasing and such 'settlers' have almost always found it to their advantage to become 'migrants'.

Marketing Problems

The settlements that could be described as successful have not been without their problems, one of the major ones being the marketing of products. Where migrants have succeeded in overcoming the difficulties involved in bringing their land under cultivation and have managed to produce more than they need for local consumption, they have often found that they cannot dispose of their excess products due to lack of marketing facilities. Bad roads, broken bridges and lack of transportation have forced them to let their crops rot. Naturally, there is no encouragement for migrants to try to increase production if they know that they cannot transport their products to a market.

In some cases this problem has arisen from the fact that the site of the project was badly selected. In most instances, however, its roots lie in the fact that the infrastructure of most areas outside Java and Bali is inadequate. The Shire of Luwu in South Sulawesi is a good example of an area where great progress could be made not just in transmigration settlements but in the whole region if better road communications were available. Proximity to markets has usually been one of the last considerations in the choice of settlement sites, which points to the fact that in the past, settlements were more or less expected to remain at a subsistence level. Quite a few of the more successful projects established in recent years could expand in a relatively short time if farmers could market their products. The former subsistence economy cannot be replaced by a cash-crop economy unless marketing facilities are adequate.

Where projects are not completely inaccessible but migrants have no way of transporting products, it usually happens that they sell to middlemen from the towns. These middlemen come into the settlements, prepared to buy whatever small quantities the settlers have for sale. With no other option, the farmer is forced to sell at a relatively low price.

Allied to this is the lack of processing facilities. Once again, migrants could obtain better prices if they had the means of processing agricultural produce like cassava. However, the migrants themselves are not well-off enough economically to finance the establishment of such facilities as tapioca factories and cassava pelletizing units.

It has always been a principle that co-operatives should be established in transmigration settlements. Writing shortly before the Second World War on the subject of resettlement of farmers from Java, Dr. Hatta had emphasized the need for co-operatives if the standard of living of migrants in new settlements was to be raised and the cycle of poverty and debt was to be broken.[14] Unfortunately, very little attention was given in the past to helping migrants establish co-operatives to handle the processing and marketing of products and to make credit available. During the First Five-Year Plan, 91 co-operatives were set up in transmigration projects, some of them as Village Enterprise Units (*B.U.U.D.*) and some as Village Unit Co-operatives (*Koperasi Unit Desa* or *K.U.D.*), in an attempt to help settlers with the marketing of products. The work of the co-operatives has so far been limited by lack of managerial skills and also lack

of financial backing, but their establishment is at least an indication of more conscious attempts to improve the farmer's financial position.

Financial Aspects

Certain financial problems have appeared frequently in past years, once again due to lack of definition of the tasks of the transmigration authority. There have tended to be two views about finance for transmigration. The first is that the transmigration authority, whether it be a department or a section of a department, should be given a large budget from which it should do everything required, including the recruiting of migrants, transportation to project areas, actual settlement work like land clearing, house construction and road building, and even the construction of small dams and weirs. Obviously this involves more than just an allocation of funds, for such a policy implies the availability of heavy equipment, engineers, and so on.

The second view is that finances for transmigration work should be given to departments like Public Works and that the transmigration authority itself should be a co-ordinating body. In past years this second view formed the basis of policies in the budget allowances given to the transmigration authority. But, as has been pointed out above, lack of satisfactory co-ordination with other government departments and agencies has been a major hindrance in settlement work. The government appeared to be reluctant to adopt the first view, possibly because of lack of conviction about the ultimate success of projects.

With the emphasis placed on transmigration in both the First and the Second Five-Year Development Plans, however, policies are changing and more funds are being made available directly to the transmigration authority itself, which is consequently less dependent upon the work of other departments. Added to this is the interest shown since 1971 in land settlement work in Indonesia by various international agencies, which have also provided considerable financial and technical assistance.

In past years repayment by migrants of money provided by the government for the activities involved in transmigration (transportation, housing, food, etc.) has made a negligible contribution to the budget of the transmigration agency. The general assumption in the past was that migrants, once productive, should commence repaying money. During the 1950s, settlers in some projects like Punggur did manage to repay a certain amount, but during the 1960s, when virtually all projects faced economic problems, or at the very least economic stagnation, the issue of repayment was dropped completely. The 1972 Act makes no reference to the matter but Clause 37 of Government Regulation No. 42 states that: 'A transmigrant is obliged to repay a part of the finance made available by the Government; the amount and method of repayment are to be regulated by a Ministerial Decision'. As yet nothing has been done about implementation of this clause. If settlers are to attain better living standards, they obviously cannot be burdened too soon with the repayment of 'loans'. But once a project is transferred to the provincial government, the transmigration agency is no longer in a position to collect 'debts'. Ultimately the government will obtain a certain financial return once the settlement reaches a reasonable level of economic growth and migrants begin paying regular taxes. Thus it would appear that, despite the Clause referred to above, the government is not intending to do anything at present about the settler's 'obligation' to repay finance.

[1] R. Soebiantoro, *Transmigration and the Prospects It Offers for Prosperity and Security*, op. cit., p. 25.

[2] Settlements were made in North Sumatra (at Pangkalan Susu) and in Kalimantan (at Pematang Tujuh and Samboja).

[3] Soebandi Resosoedarmo, 'Perundang-Undangan Transmigrasi' (Transmigration Legislation) in *Arti dan Peranan Transmigrasi di Indonesia*, op. cit., p. 108.

[4] *Garis-Garis Besar Rentjana Pembangunan Lima Tahun 1956–1960*, op. cit., p. 64.

[5] A problem of this kind arose as recently as 1971, when the transmigration authority had to pay compensation for 5 hectares of rubber trees planted by local people on land made available for a project at Tekam/Mempawah in West Kalimantan. *Laporan Tahunan Tahun ke-3*, op. cit., p. 12.

[6] It is worth noting, however, that with the increasingly systematic collection of the Regional Development Tax known as IPEDA (*Iuran Pembangunan Daerah*) in rural areas outside Java, shifting cultivators are becoming more wary about laying claim to ownership of any land other than that under cultivation.

[7] *Pola Kerdja Sama Departemen Transkopemada Dengan Departemen-Departemen Lain*, op. cit., pp. 40-1.

[8] *Contribution to the Realization of the Transmigration Projects*, Forestry Department, Ministry of Agriculture (Jakarta, 1966), pp. 3-4.

[9] *Kumpulan Reportase Pengawalan dan Survey Transmigrasi Tahun 1967*, op. cit., p. 41.

[10] *Transmigrasi, Koperasi dan Pembangunan Masjarakat Desa 1959–1962*, Department of Transmigration, Co-operatives and Rural Community Development (Jakarta, 1962), p. 18.

[11] Soedigdo Hardjosudarmo, op. cit., p. 90, footnote 34.

[12] N. Daldjoeni, 'Dua Visi Tentang Pendekatan Kulturil di Daerah Transmigrasi' in *Kompas*, 20 January 1973.

[13] *Punggur–Daerah Transmigrasi Dengan Pola Pertanian Sawah Beririgasi*, Pusat Latihan dan Penelitian Transmigrasi (Jakarta, 1974), p. 34.

[14] Mohammad Hatta, 'Koperasi dasar transmigrasi, bukan feodalisme' (The co-operative, not feudalism, as the basis for transmigration), in *Beberapa Fasal Ekonomi*, Vol. I, 4th edition, Balai Pustaka (Jakarta, 1950), p. 79.

V
Success and Failure – Sumatra

Projects in Lampung

SINCE the first days of colonization by the Dutch in the early twentieth century, southern Sumatra has always formed the main settlement area in programmes to move people from Java. The obvious advantage of this region is its proximity to Java, which has always made communications relatively easy. The railway line from Jakarta to Merak links up with a ferry that carries passengers, vehicles and goods across the Sunda Strait to Panjang. From Panjang a railway line runs north across Lampung to Palembang, the capital of South Sumatra. After independence, transmigration undertakings tended to continue Dutch colonization plans, which, as pointed out in an earlier chapter, were concentrated in Lampung and South Sumatra. The emphasis upon this region was continued in the early 1960s, for the Eight-Year Plan of 1961–1969 had stated that resettlement work was to be focused upon southern Sumatra 'to obtain the maximum results with the minimum expense.'[1] During the Five-Year Development Plan of 1969–1974, most of the migrants settled in Sumatra went to the southern provinces of the island, as Table 10 shows.

Quite apart from colonization and transmigration programmes, there has always been a steady movement of people from Java to southern Sumatra, the effect of which upon the composition of the population of Lampung is quite apparent. The 1930 census indicated that 36·2 per cent of the total Lampung population of 361 000 consisted of people from different parts of Java. In 1971, however, two-thirds of the population, placed by the census of that year at 2 777 085, consisted of non-indigenous people. The difference is explained by the movement into the province not just of government-sponsored migrants but also of independent settlers who have migrated of their own accord.

Between 1952 and 1968, 24 transmigration projects were established in Lampung (Table 11). Seventeen of them had already been transferred to the provincial government by the end of 1970; of these, fourteen have, with some rearrangement of project boundaries and the inclusion of non-project land, become *kecamatan* (administrative districts). Of the projects still under the care of the Directorate-General for Transmigration, one, Seputih Surabaya, has also become a *kecamatan*. In 1973–4 a project was opened in the Panaragan area as an extension of the Way Abung project, bringing the total amount of land used for transmigration purposes in Lampung to almost 300 000 hectares.

In the period between 1952 and the end of October 1973, 259 726 people were placed in transmigration settlements in Lampung. However, the total population of these settlements was already 555 520 in October 1973, as the result of natural increase, the placing of settlers in project areas by other government agencies, the movement into projects by completely unsponsored migrants (of whom accurate records were never kept), and the settlement of local indigenous people in projects.[2] In the years between 1952 and 1973 other agencies, mainly the Department of Social Welfare and the Armed Forces, settled another 33 379 migrants in Lampung in projects of their own.

During the First Five-Year Plan of 1969–1974, 52 377 migrants (half of the number who went to Sumatra) were settled in Lampung. Of these, 31 984 people were moved during 1973–4 under General Transmigration or Independent Transmigration with Assistance. Most of the migrants moved during this five-year period went to the Way

Table 10
Migrants Settled in Sumatra by Project, 1969–1974

Project	1969–70	1970–1	1971–2	1972–3	1973–4	Total
Balau Kedaton	3 095	572				
Way Abung/ Panaragan	1 596	1 717	2 952	10 461	24 833	
Older projects					7 151	
Lampung						52 377
Belitang	1 739	2 645	708	9 697		
Delta Upang	728	1 357	884	2 409		
Cintamanis			1 841		4 050	
Air Deras	464	224		455		
Air Beliti	890			1 898		
South Sumatra						29 989
Bukit Peninjauan				1 814	1 934	
Pekik Nyaring				1 918		
Rimbo Kedui		469				
Bengkulu						6 135
Rantau Rasau	1 733	1 366	1 882	3 131	3 267	
Jambi						11 379
Simandolak	867					
Teluk Kiambang			735		737	
Riau						2 339
Sei Tambangan					772	
Lunang					1 339	
West Sumatra						2 111
Aek Naetek					894	
North Sumatra						894
SUMATRA	11 112	8 350	9 002	31 783	44 977	105 224

Source: Directorate-General for Transmigration, Jakarta.

Note: Figures for 1973–4 include people settled up to 13 April, 1974.

Abung/Panaragan projects. In the fifth year, however, when it became obvious that these two projects could not accommodate all the people to be settled in Lampung, the provincial government of Lampung decided to place migrants in older projects that had already been transferred from the authority of the transmigration agency to the local government administration.[3] A further 7 503 people moved to Lampung in 1973–4 under the *Banpres* and Unassisted Independent Transmi-

gration programmes, more than half of them going to older projects.

Experiences in Lampung in the last two years of the First Five-Year Plan, when comparatively large numbers of migrants were moved to the same projects, emphasized that attempts to differentiate between *umum* and assisted *spontan* migrants achieve no purpose. The people who moved as *umum* or general migrants received cleared land, houses already built, tools, kitchen utensils, clothing, seed

Table 11
Transmigration Projects in Lampung, 1952–March 1973

Project	Period of settlement	Project area (ha)	Population (1973)	Year of transfer
I. SOUTH LAMPUNG				
1. Palas	1958–73	14 300	15 127	1970*
2. Sidomulyo	1958–73	14 500	27 053	1970*
3. Balau Kedaton	1961–73	12 000	7 041	1970
4. Sidomakmur	1967	500	977	
5. Tanjungan	1968–73	1 000	1 867	
		42 300	52 065	
II. CENTRAL LAMPUNG				
6. Sekampung	1952–5	3 000	18 069	1955*
7. Purbolinggo	1952–6	10 000	46 704	1963*
8. Punggur	1953–7	10 000	33 013	1968*
9. Pekalongan	1953–7	1 000	8 711	1963
10. Lb. Maringgai	1953–6	142	3 023	1956
11. Sept. Raman	1954–9	12 630	46 915	1968*
12. Raman Utara	1955–8	9 958	28 655	1968*
13. Way Seputih	1954–61	10 537·5	57 172	1968*
14. Seputih Banyak	1958–61	19 180	44 752	1969*
15. Rumbia Barat/ Sept. Buminabung	1960–72	9 738	20 537	1969*
16. Way Jepara	1957–63	11 658	46 255	1968*
17. Sept. Mataram	1962–5	38 000	43 229	1969*
18. Lempuyang	1959	12 000	732	
19. Banjaratu	1959–63	6 000	4 209	
20. Sept. Surabaya	1965–70	10 000	11 045	*
		163 843·5	413 021	
III. NORTH LAMPUNG				
21. Baradatu	1959–63	17 500	19 906	1970*
22. Banjit	1952–63		19 303	1970*
23. Negeri Agung	1965	8 500	8 542	
24. Way Abung	1965–73	20 000	29 138	
		46 000	76 889	
TOTAL LAMPUNG :		252 143·5	541 975	

Source: *Laporan Tahunan Tahun Kerja 1972/1973*, Direktorat Transmigrasi, Propinsi Lampung (Tanjungkarang, 1973), pp. 43-4.

Note: Projects marked * are now administrative districts (*kecamatan*).

and basic necessities (rice, salted fish, salt, cooking oil and kerosene for lamps) for one year. The *spontan* migrants received land that in most cases was not cleared, as well as basic necessities for two months. Some migrants received a small quantity of seed. In keeping with past policy, the *umum* migrants were all sent to the newest project, Panaragan, where settlement work would be the hardest. In actual fact, however, large numbers of *spontan* migrants who received comparatively little assistance were also settled in Panaragan. Even those who went to older projects already transferred, such as Palas and Banjit, found it hard to get established on their holdings with the small amount of assistance they received. The *spontan* migrants who moved without any financial assistance from the government (*tanpa bantuan biaya*) were helped by the Makarti Mukti Tama Foundation. They received only 2 hectares of land and paid all expenses involved in moving from Java and in settling in Lampung. The Directorate-General for Transmigration has therefore decided to do away with distinctions between different categories of migrants as from April 1974 and to provide all with the same facilities.

Most of the projects established in Lampung between 1952 and 1968 were really extensions of existing Dutch colonization projects, while others were established on sites previously selected and, in some cases, surveyed by the Dutch colonization authority. The intention was that irrigation should be made available, for the basic concept in colonization in Lampung had been the cultivation of wet rice as in Java. This explains why development has varied considerably from one project to another. Those settlements which, like Sekampung, obtained irrigation very soon after migrants arrived have followed the colonization pattern in almost all respects. Farmers have obtained good yields of rice from their fields but levels of prosperity have remained low. The settlements have become overcrowded and the fragmentation of holdings has occurred in most areas, for no land was left for natural expansion. Farmers have not been able to grow commercial crops because their farms are too small, and hence they have had no additional source of income.

Those projects that were planned as irrigated-rice areas but were not provided with irrigation water soon after settlement began have fared rather badly. Settlers have had to depend on one crop of dry rice each year, with cassava as their main crop. In fact, in many places farmers have been able to grow only cassava, for yields of dry rice have decreased constantly. The results of lack of coordination between plans made for the settlement of migrants and plans for the provision of irrigation facilities are apparent in many of these projects, where it has been necessary to carry out rehabilitation work in the period since 1969. The Lampung Public Works Office, which is responsible for irrigation in the province, has pointed out:

It is clear that if a transmigration plan is started at the same time as an irrigation plan, the irrigation plan will lag behind, due to the faster planning and placement of the transmigrants.[4]

Experiences in the Way Seputih area of Central Lampung have shown only too well the truth of this statement.

The Way Seputih project was established in 1954 on land that had been transferred by the local *marga* to the Dutch colonial government in 1941 for colonization purposes. Government-sponsored migrants were placed in the project up to 1961, after which numbers of independent migrants settled there of their own accord. In the years from 1954 to 1961, 19 202 people were placed in the twelve villages of the Way Seputih project, which had a total area of 10 537·5 hectares. The project, despite its lack of economic growth, was transferred to the local provincial government in April 1968, and now forms the greater part of the District of Terbanggi Besar, with the town of Bandarjaya as the *kecamatan* administrative centre. Hence it is no longer the responsibility of the Directorate-General for Transmigration.

When this project was first established, the intention was that irrigation would be made available for about 25 000 hectares of land in the area drained by the Way Seputih, as stated in the Five-Year Plan for 1956–1960. But although the irrigation scheme was begun in 1956, work was discontinued shortly after-

Map 2: Lampung: transmigration settlements, 1950–1974

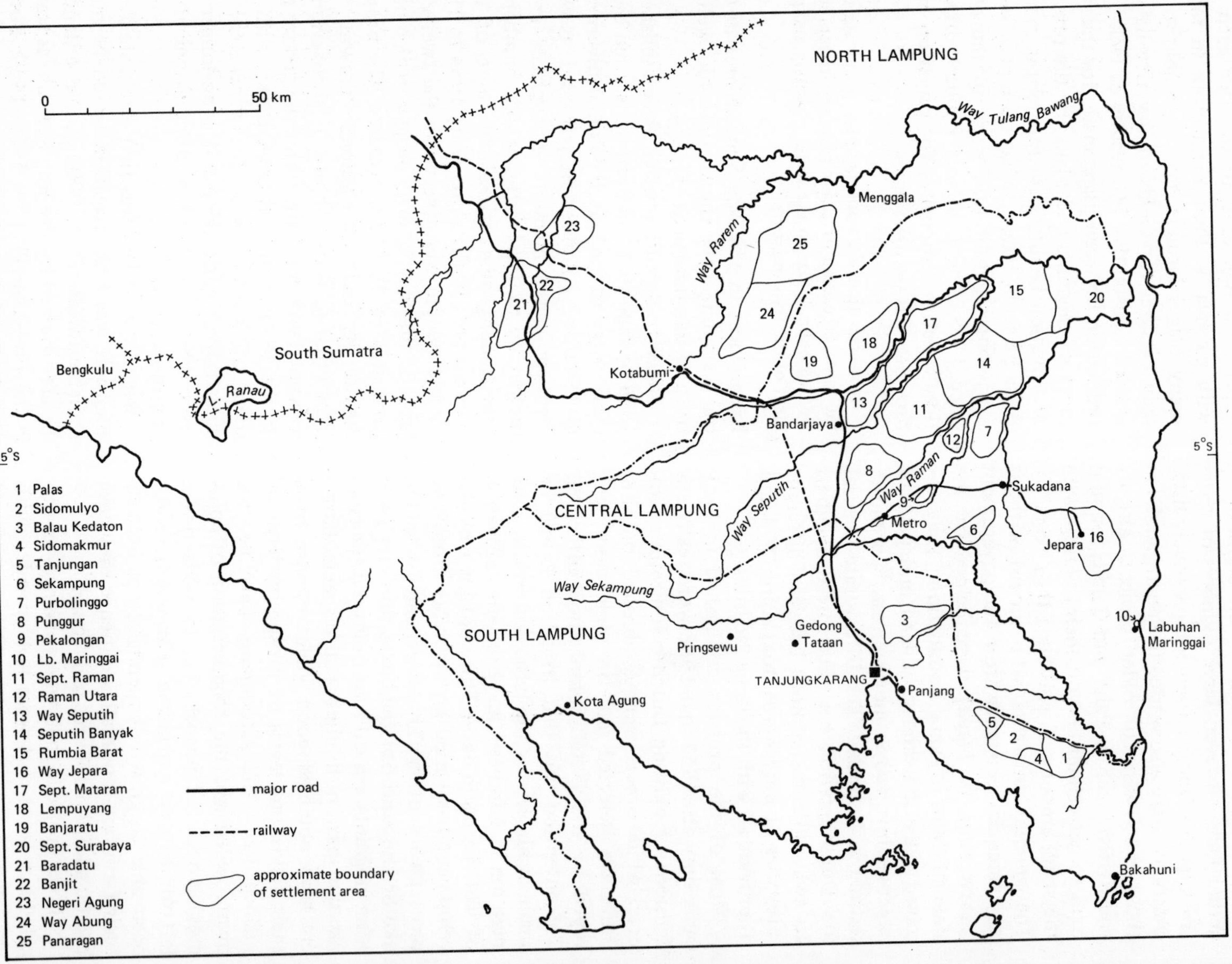

50

5°S

NORTH LAMPUNG

CENTRAL LAMPUNG

SOUTH LAMPUNG

South Sumatra

Bengkulu

Way Tulang Bawang

Way Rarem

Way Rarem

Way Seputih

Way Seputih

Way Sekampung

Way Raman

Ranau

Mengala

Kotabumi

Bandarjaya

Metro

Sukadana

Jepara

Labuhan Maringgai

Bakahuni

Panjang

TANJUNGKARANG

Gedong

Tataan

Pringsewu

Kota Agung

50 km

0

major road

railway

approximate boundary of settlement area

1 Palas
2 Sidomulyo
3 Balau Kedaton
4 Sidomakmur
5 Tanjungan
6 Sekampung
7 Purbolinggo
8 Punggur
9 Pekalongan
10 Lb. Maringgai
11 Sept. Raman
12 Raman Utara
13 Way Seputih
14 Seputih Banyak
15 Rumbia Barat
16 Way Jepara
17 Sept. Mataram
18 Lempuyang
19 Banjaratu
20 Sept. Surabaya
21 Baradatu
22 Banjit
23 Negeri Agung
24 Way Abung
25 Panaragan

5°S

wards, and migrants were forced to obtain a very inadequate livelihood from the cultivation of cassava and other dry crops. In 1968 work on the irrigation project was resumed with help from the International Bank for Reconstruction and Development.

Over the years the population of the Way Seputih area has increased considerably; in March 1973 there were 57 172 people living in the original project area for, despite the lack of irrigation, independent settlers moved into this area and into the adjacent Seputih Mataram settlement (known also as Way Seputih II), which in 1973 had 43 229 people on the 12 644 hectares of cultivated land in the original project area. In addition to these settlements, two small Army projects, Poncowati I (1964) and Poncowati II (1970), were also established close to the Seputih projects in the expectation that irrigation water would be available. In all cases groups of local people remained within the project areas.

When the major part of the irrigation system was ready in 1973, farmers could not benefit immediately for the land had not been prepared for the cultivation of wet rice. Dry crops had been grown continuously for several years and, with no immediate prospect of irrigation water, farmers had not levelled their land or dyked the fields. Similarly, the tertiary canals and the smaller channels to carry water to individual fields had not been dug, for farmers were unwilling to undertake this heavy work until they felt certain that the primary and secondary canals would be constructed by the Public Works Department. The matter was further complicated by problems involving land ownership and lack of capital.

In the years between the original settlement of migrants in the Way Seputih area and 1968, when the irrigation project was recommenced, much buying and selling of land took place in an unregistered fashion. Many migrants who had originally been allocated land, feeling doubtful that the government would keep to its plans for irrigation, simply abandoned their holdings or else sold them to local people or to more optimistic unsponsored migrants. Others, however, purchased additional land from local people living within the project area. Since no land deeds were ever issued to the original migrants, it has been extremely difficult to determine the genuine claimants to the land. Disputes have occurred in several villages.

Apart from the issue of land claims, a further problem, not anticipated when the irrigation scheme was recommenced, has arisen. A certain amount of capital is required to convert dry fields into irrigated fields. The farmers, migrants and local people alike, who remained on the land, have not been in a position to save money, for their life has been very much at a subsistence level. In some places it has been necessary to clear the land again, for *alang-alang* grass and scrub have appeared. The fact that many of the migrants were comparatively advanced in years when the irrigation scheme was completed and so did not have the physical strength to undertake the heavy work of clearing, levelling and dyking their land, has formed another aspect of the problem. Furthermore, not all farmers had the necessary technical skill required for the task of converting land to wet-rice cultivation.

In view of the need to make full use of all potential rice land, the government decided to make available to those farmers whose land claims were quite clear the capital needed for the conversion of fields to wet-rice production.[5] In an attempt to speed up this work, the World Food Programme began providing food at the end of 1972 to enable farmers in Way Seputih and the nearby Punggur area to undertake the digging of tertiary canals, the levelling and dyking of fields and rehabilitation and construction of roads. A total of 4 600 families in Way Seputih and 2 500 families in Punggur have received help in the form of food.[6] Unfortunately, there is now some doubt as to whether the Way Seputih can supply enough water for the total area of 25 000 hectares originally to be irrigated. Reforestation in the catchment area of the Way Seputih has been commenced, but at the present time it appears that only 15 000 hectares can be irrigated. In the parts where wet-rice cultivation has begun, farmers can obtain a crop of wet rice only in the wet season and are still dependent upon dry crops (mainly corn) for their dry-season income.

One further aspect, significant for future project planning, is the fact that when the Way Seputih project was first established, no allowance was made for expansion within the project itself, which today is comparatively densely populated. No attempt was made to keep reserve land for the children of the original settlers, for animal grazing or for the cultivation of cash crops. Lack of land has made it impossible for farmers to rotate crops in an effort to preserve soil fertility, though it must be admitted that farmers in this and the other projects established during the 1950s and the 1960s never received any guidance from agricultural extension workers in such matters.

The Way Seputih project illustrates many of the mistakes made in transmigration settlements in past years. The whole project was originally planned as an irrigated-rice settlement but failure to make water available in the early years forced migrants to turn to the cultivation of cassava when they found that dry-rice yields were too low to warrant the labour required. There has been very little economic growth in the area and today, twenty years after the first migrants were settled, the government, with the assistance of the international agencies already mentioned, has been obliged to make large inputs of money and facilities in an attempt to rehabilitate the settlements in the area.

A similar situation has occurred in the Punggur project, which was originally planned as an extension of the Sekampung and Purbolinggo projects. When settlement began in 1953 it was intended that irrigation would be available when extensions to the canal network to the north of the Way Sekampung were completed. But although work was com-

menced in 1959, very little was accomplished and migrants were forced to rely on cassava as yields of dry rice and corn decreased steadily. Farmers in the village of Sritejo Kencono, the most prosperous of the fifteen villages in the Punggur project, obtained 1·0 tonne of rice per hectare in the first years of settlement, but by the 1960s this had dropped to 0·4 tonne per hectare, while corn yields had declined from 0·5 to 0·2 tonne per hectare over the same period.[7] The establishment of a tapioca factory in Sritejo Kencono for the processing of locally grown cassava is perhaps the main reason for the greater economic progress of this village. When irrigation was finally made available in 1971–2, the same problems arose as in Way Seputih. Tertiary canals had to be constructed and fields levelled and dyked. Fortunately land tenure problems were better controlled. Migrants had not been given ownership titles; only usage rights had been granted. Local district-level authorities prohibited all land transactions and also the use of land as collateral to obtain credit until proper registration had taken place, for when irrigation finally became a reality there were signs that land disputes similar to those in Way Seputih would arise. When it was definite that water would be available, there was a rise in population as more completely unsponsored settlers moved to the area. According to the 1971 census the population of Punggur was 30 408 in that year, but in June 1974 it was 39 097.

The Department of Agriculture introduced the *Bimas* intensification programme in the Punggur area in the 1972–3 planting season and in the Way Seputih area in the 1973–4 season; farmers whose fields were already levelled and dyked could obtain *Bimas* assistance for the cultivation of wet rice. Yields in the first season in Punggur were poor but in the 1973–4 season farmers obtained an average of more than 2 tonnes per hectare from the 2 409 hectares under irrigated rice. With the successful implementation of *Bimas*, there will be an input of better quality seed, as well as fertilizers and pesticides, which should result in higher yields and hence an increase in farm incomes.

Bearing in mind experiences in Way Seputih and Punggur, which are by no means isolated cases though probably the most serious in terms of acreage and numbers of settlers involved, the transmigration authority has, in the years since 1969, given attention to the development of dry farming in the seven projects still under its care in Lampung. Of these, the Way Abung and Panaragan projects in North Lampung are by far the largest.

The first villages (Tatakarya and Purbasakti) in the Way Abung project were established in 1965 at the time of the National Transmigration Movement. The original settlement was made with 4 927 independent migrants, who received only a small amount of assistance at the time of arrival in Lampung. In 1967 another 991 people were settled in Way Abung, but of the original migrants 2 659 have left the project area, which covers 20 000 hectares. In 1969, when it was found that migrants scheduled for placement in tidal projects could not be settled because of inadequate preparation of the canal networks, Way Abung was selected as one of the four projects for the 1969–70 Crash Program. In the years between 1969 and March 1974, 41 559 migrants were placed in this project and in the adjacent Panaragan project, which has an area of 33 800 hectares. Independent migrants have also settled in the two projects, which in August 1974 had a total population of 50 409.

Because of land problems, only 30 000 hectares out of the total 53 800 hectares in the two projects can be used. When the original survey work was done, certain 'enclaves' of land were left for local people, some of whom were shifting cultivators while others had small rubber holdings. When settlement work was commenced, however, it turned out that local people held more land than was originally estimated. This, together with the fact that there was a certain amount of overlapping with land held by private companies operating

in the field of agriculture, has reduced the amount of land available for migrants. By the end of the First Five-Year Plan, 20 782 hectares had been allocated to the 11 161 families in the two projects; of this, 10 205 hectares were under cultivation. A survey made in 1974 found that the area is already overcrowded and that there is no room for further expansion, a situation made more critical by the fact that settlers are dependent upon dry farming, for which more than 2 hectares per family is desirable.[8]

The original settlements made in Way Abung in 1965 have, like similar non-irrigated projects in Lampung, been feeling the effects of soil deterioration, as a consequence of almost continuous cassava cultivation. The Department of Public Works has plans for irrigation in this area, using water from the Way Rarem.[9] However, attention is being given to the improvement of dry farming in the two projects, for past experiences have shown that it may be some years before irrigation water actually appears. Farmers have followed the *tumpang sari* system of intercropping, common in those parts of Java where water is not available for a second rice crop in the dry season. Dry rice is grown (one crop a year), along with corn (two crops a year in most parts of the project) and cassava. In some places soya beans are also cultivated, while wet rice is grown in the limited swamp areas within the project. So far, farmers have not begun cultivating cash crops.

The *Bimas* intensification programme was introduced in Way Abung in the 1973–4 planting season. In previous years *Bimas* facilities were not provided for the cultivation of non-irrigated crops. Results were disappointing, however, for a variety of reasons. The *Bimas* supplies of seed and fertilizer arrived later than expected. Rain did not fall at the usual time, which in the comparatively dry Way Abung area meant further problems. Moreover, the farmers themselves did not really understand the methods required for successful intensification, due to insufficient extension work at the field level. Farmers in the eight villages where *Bimas* was introduced on 1 075 hectares under dry rice and 281 hectares under corn found that average yields were no better than in previous years (0·8 tonne of rice and 0·5 tonne of corn per hectare).

Observations in Way Abung have indicated that it takes four to five years for a migrant family to bring the 2 hectares allocated per family under cultivation.[10] Lack of both labour and money is the main reason, plus the fact that tools are very limited. Also, migrants have no draught animals to assist them in the preparation of fields. Incomes begin to improve once the family has all its land under cultivation, even though cassava, the major crop, brings relatively low returns. More attention has been given to animal husbandry in Way Abung than in older projects, but few settlers are in a position to purchase animals, at least during their first three or four years in the project. In view of the poor soils in the Way Abung area, further expansion of mixed farming is desirable, for soils would benefit from animal manure. At the same time, the sale of animal products would mean additional income for farmers.

Difficulty in marketing still imposes limitations upon economic expansion in Way Abung and Panaragan. Transportation costs from the projects to market centres are extremely high, partly because of the poor condition of the roads that link settlements to the main provincial roads and partly because project co-operatives are not yet able to function effectively. World Food Programme has provided food for 2 500 families in Way Abung and 1 800 families in Panaragan to enable work to be undertaken on the urgently needed infrastructure, as well as on the preparation of dry fields. The proximity of the project to Kotabumi, the capital of North Lampung, through which both the main road and the railway line to Palembang pass, will be a greater advantage than at present, once a better road has been constructed to link the projects with the town.

Twelve Village Unit Co-operatives have been established in Way Abung and Panaragan in an attempt to provide farmers with the inputs they require and to help them with the marketing of products. The lack of management skills and capital, however, has made it difficult for co-operatives to function well, and the marketing process is still dominated by middlemen who, since the first days of the original settlements, have provided the only transportation available for settlers to sell their small surplus of agricultural products, timber and charcoal. Some progress was made in 1973–4 when the co-operatives, using credit extended by the Kotabumi branch of the Indonesian People's Bank, were able to purchase rice and dried cassava from farmers at prices higher than those offered by middlemen. Prices received by farmers for their products have remained low for, apart from high transportation costs, the quality of products is poor as a consequence of bad processing. The complexity of the problem can be seen from a recent attempt to assist migrants in the marketing of cassava. Permission was given early in 1974 for a pelletizing company to operate in the project area in conjunction with the Village Unit Co-operatives, which were to supply the company with dried cassava. The company, however, has purchased fresh cassava directly from farmers, thus by-passing the co-operatives.[11] The farmers received very low prices but were presumably influenced by the cash payment offered by the company. In general, confidence in co-operatives is still limited but with better management and provision of credit by external sources at the time when it is needed, the co-operatives should be able to play a greater role in marketing in future years.

Attention has been given in Way Abung and Panaragan to the establishment of an administrative system in each of the twenty village units in the projects, so as to facilitate transfer to the provincial administration when project status ceases. To help in the development of a competent village administration, village officials have been appointed within a year after settlement and they are trained by transmigration staff in the routine tasks of village administration and the keeping of proper records. Special courses have also been conducted in an attempt to develop competent leadership at the village level. Village facilities that include a central administrative office, a meeting hall and a community granary have been provided in each village unit.

Although population density in Lampung was 82 to the sq km in 1971 (the second highest figure for provinces in Sumatra), distribution is very uneven. The Shires of South and Central Lampung are far more densely populated than is the Shire of North Lampung as a consequence of the concentration of Dutch colonization settlements in the southern part of the province. Even in 1950 and 1951 farmers originally from Java were migrating northwards from the Gedong Tataan and Pringsewu areas.[12] In 1972 the Sumatra Regional Planning Study found evidence of the same trend, as was pointed out by a member of the survey team:

Our survey of 250 farmers in the Pringsewu area shows that 35—40% of the population in the age group of 18—25 years has already emigrated again. . . . After thirty years of hard labour the Javanese immigrants are finding that their grandchildren again have no land to cultivate and again young farmers are forced to leave their villages.[13]

Therefore the transmigration authority is planning to locate future projects in North Lampung, leaving such land as is still unoccupied in the southern shires for the natural expansion of existing settlements, which offer possibilities for further intensification, assuming that irrigation is provided. With the use of better quality seed, fertilizers and insecticides, and with better water management where irrigation already exists, productivity could be greatly increased. This, however, is the task of other government departments, for almost all of these projects have been transferred to the provincial government.

The large areas of land as yet unused in North Lampung can best be utilized, as far as transmigration is concerned, for dry farming. A large percentage of the migrants scheduled for placement in Lampung during the Second Five-Year Plan will go to a new project to be established close to the town of Menggala. With the implementation of the policies formulated during the First Five-Year Plan, there is every expectation that the new village units to be established in Lampung will be more than the 'cassava villages' of the past.

Projects in South Sumatra

The Province of South Sumatra, adjacent to Lampung, has never had the number of transmigration projects established in the latter province. The early settlements in the 1950s were extensions of the Dutch colonization projects at Belitang and Tugumulyo. It was to the Belitang area and the Metro area in Lampung that most of the migrants moved under 'family' and 'general' transmigration in the 1950—4 period went. Of the 37 744 people living in Belitang in 1954, 24 627 had moved in the years after 1950.[14] The project was officially handed over to the provincial government in 1962, but since that time completely unsponsored migrants, attracted by its comparative prosperity, have continued to move into the district. During the First Five-Year Plan of 1969–1974 the transmigration agency established four new villages in the vicinity of Belitang for 14 789 partly assisted migrants, who received only transportation and uncleared land.

The Belitang project is a good example of the pattern that can be established in transmigration, given certain basic advantages. The original site was well chosen; the soil was comparatively good and water was available from the Komering and Belitang Rivers. With the extensions made since 1950 to the irrigation network partly constructed by the Dutch government in 1941, the area has continued to prosper, one further advantage being its location 55 km from the town of Martapura.

Map 3:   Central and northern Sumatra: major transmigration settlements, 1950–1974

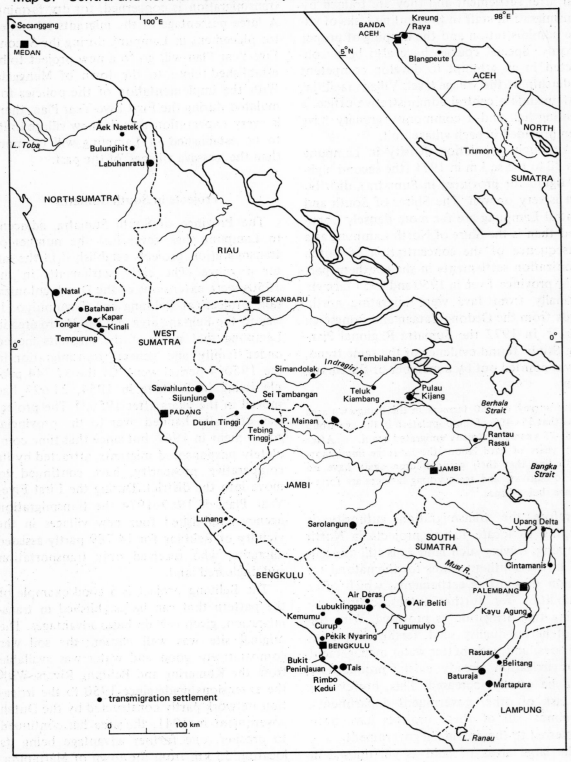

Marketing of products has never presented the insurmountable problems that it has in other transmigration settlements. With improvement of the provincial roads that link the settlement area with Martapura and with Rasuan and Kayu Agung, farmers have been able to sell their agricultural and home-industry products outside the local area. Although marketing could be further improved with an effective system of co-operatives, settlers are relatively well off and Belitang is now a rice-surplus area. In a province where most local farmers cultivate smallholder rubber, there is constant demand for rice and other foodstuffs. Independent migrants have been attracted to the Belitang area, just as they have to the Sukadana-Sekampung area in Lampung. Of the 7 314 *Banpres* programme migrants who settled in South Sumatra in the first half of 1974, 4 018 went to Rasuan and Kertanegara in the Belitang area. Adjustment over the years since 1950 has proved no problem since newcomers have fitted into a pattern of irrigated farming with which they are familiar. Once again, however, there has been virtually no assimilation between migrants and the local people of the area.

Other small projects established in South Sumatra between 1950 and 1968 have done less well, due mainly to the fact that settlements were small and scattered. These projects (Taman Agung, Karang Menjangan, Way Hitam Baru and Cahaya Tani), where 3 377 families were originally settled, are to be transferred to the local government in June 1975; no migrants have been placed in them since 1967 and lack of progress has discouraged independent settlers. Present policies are directed towards larger settlements so that greater benefit can be obtained from the money invested in settlement work.

Between 1969 and 1974, the Directorate-General for Transmigration settled 12 779 general migrants and 2 421 partly assisted migrants in four new projects in South Sumatra. Of these people 3 931 went to Air Deras and Air Beliti, which were established in 1969

some miles from the Tugumulyo project. Air Beliti, one of the hastily prepared Crash Program projects, suffered initial setbacks because of land disputes. Migrants were originally settled on 3 500 hectares of land, 80 per cent of which later turned out to be rubber gardens owned by local smallholders. After discussion with provincial authorities and the local people, it was decided to retain the locally owned land as 'enclaves' within the transmigration project; the provincial government made another 2 000 hectares available in the same area for the migrants who had to be shifted.[15] Almost 1 000 of the 1974 *Banpres* migrants went to Air Beliti, which, together with Air Deras, is to be transferred to the provincial government in 1975.

Of special note are the tidal projects established in the Upang Delta area and at Cintamanis during the First Five-Year Plan. Although South Sumatra, with a population of 3 443 749 in 1971, had a density of only 33 to the sq km in that year, agricultural expansion is limited by the swamps that cover 21 per cent of the province. However, the fact that there is a tidal influence in many rivers has encouraged cultivators, particularly those who have moved of their own accord from southern Kalimantan, to attempt the cultivation of rice in swamp lands. When it was decided prior to the commencement of the First Five-Year Development Plan to settle migrants from Java in tidal areas, two sites were chosen in South Sumatra.

Tidal irrigation depends upon the tidal influence in river estuaries and tributaries to supply river water for irrigated fields. When the water level in the river rises, water can be channelled onto the fields. When the tide goes down, the excess water can be drained back into the river. Although the technique resembles that used for the cultivation of rice in areas where seasonal floods occur, it is more effective in that tidal influences are more regular and can be calculated in advance, whereas river floods cannot be predicted in time or extent. On the other hand, soil acidity

Map 4:   The Upang Delta settlement: sketch of canal network

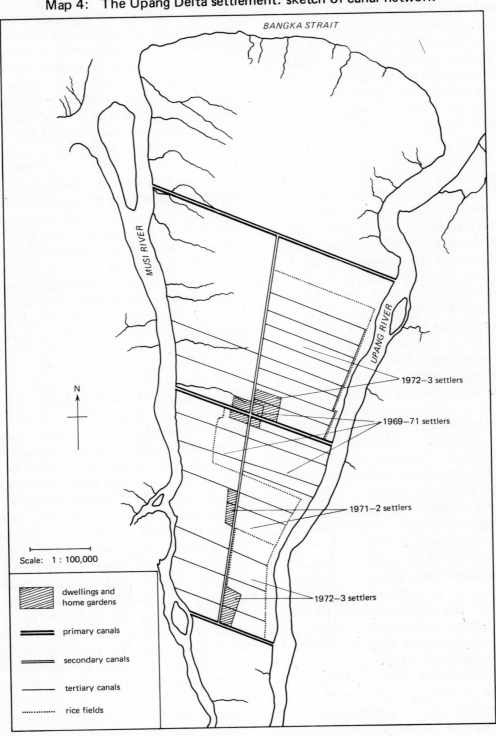

Source: Ikhtisar Keadaan Proyek-Proyek Transmigrasi
Prop. Sumatera Selatan, Enc. I., Palembang, 1973

is often a problem in tidal areas, where peat soils are frequently found.

Originally only land along river banks could be used for tidal irrigation but farmers found that by digging a series of channels more or less at right angles to the river they could spread the tidal effect further inland. In cases like the Upang Delta project where they were able to link up two rivers by means of a canal, better use could be made of tidal influences. Such cultivators, like those who grow rice in *lebak* fields along river bends and depend upon floods for water, have always found that drainage is their major problem. It is relatively easy to channel water onto the fields but special ditches must be dug so that water can be drained off the rice fields at the appropriate times. Thus a double system of channels is needed, one for the supply of water and the other for drainage. Embankments are usually made along the supply channels so that excess water does not flood the fields. In Kalimantan a kind of storage pool or tank is constructed at the ends of the secondary canals for the exchange of water and hence the same canals can be used for both supply and drainage.

The Upang Delta project is located in the Shire of Musi Banyu Asin, about 60 km downstream from Palembang. Some miles from the mouth, the Musi River branches and enters the Bangka Strait via the Musi itself and the Upang River. The project is situated on the long, narrow strip of land that forms an island between the two rivers, at a point where the tidal range is between 115 and 280 cm.[16] The total project area covers 15 000 hectares, but of this only 4 800 hectares is suited to agriculture. The settlement has progressed rapidly in a short time, largely because the soil in the interior of the island, where the four project villages are located, has benefited from alluvial deposits. Local shifting cultivators have cleared land in other parts of the island, but they have found that where the organic material in the soil is less than 10 cm in depth, permanent fields cannot be established.

During the 1969–74 period, 5 378 migrants were settled in the Delta Upang project and by mid-1974, 2 319 hectares of irrigated fields were under cultivation. So far, only rice is being grown; migrants have found that secondary crops do not do well and that it is more profitable to fell trees and sell logs and timber to obtain additional income. Marketing presents no problems; at high tide boats can enter the project area, bringing in consumer goods and carrying out rice and wood for sale in Palembang. A rice huller has already been set up, along with 24 small sawmills and 9 tile-making units.

The migrants settled in the Upang Delta have faced certain problems found in all tidal projects. First has been that of adjustment to the new environment, which in no way resembles anything farmers have been familiar with in Java, Madura or Bali. It takes several seasons for them to learn the techniques of tidal cultivation. Another problem is the lack of fresh water for household purposes in the dry season. The need for a proper supply of water was made very clear when an outbreak of cholera occurred in the Upang project in August 1972.[17] Malaria, too, is a constant problem. Migrants have also found that from the first year their crops have been troubled by rodents and wild pigs, as well as by a variety of insects, that live in the nearby forests.

The ultimate test will be the capacity of soils to continue producing satisfactory results. In the 1973–4 season, farmers obtained 3·6 tonnes of dry, unhulled rice per hectare, without fertilizers. However, only one rice crop can be obtained per year, since rice varieties cultivated in tidal areas are of the long-growing type, which means that farmers really need an additional source of income. If fertility can be maintained with the use of fertilizers, the project should continue to prosper. Since water is available for most of the year, it is possible that two crops could be obtained if varieties of rice common in Java were used. However, experiments have shown that average yields from such varieties, if grown in tidal areas, are low. Farmers have already discovered that there must be no transfer of the lower layers of clay to the surface, since the clay has a high acidity. Where embankments have been made along canals by digging out clay from the canals, nothing can be cultivated because of its acidity.[18] More serious is the problem of sedimentation. There is already evidence that siltation is making the canals shallow.[19] This has been found to be a major problem in all tidal-irrigation projects, for once drainage is impeded the irrigation system cannot function properly.

This problem of acidity is more in evidence in the second of the tidal projects, that established at Cintamanis on the Salak River. Local soils are not very fertile and drainage has increased acidity. Migrants have been unable to obtain satisfactory rice crops and so have turned to the cultivation of cassava. Yields from the newly cleared land have been high enough to interest the provincial government in the establishment of a tapioca pelletizing factory. But for such a factory to become a profitable venture, production of cassava would have to be greatly increased, and this would be possible only if a far greater area of land in the vicinity of the present project was settled and cultivated. In 1971–2, the first year of settlement, 1 841 people were placed at Cintamanis, while in 1973–4 all of the 4 050 migrants who moved to South Sumatra were settled at Cintamanis in an attempt to stimulate economic growth in the area.

Apart from the extensive swamp lands, South Sumatra still has land available for future settlements. During the Second Five-Year Development Plan attention is to be given to the establishment of dry-farming projects in the southern part of this province, particularly in the Pematang Panggang area, where smallholder cultivation of rubber is already significant in local land-use patterns.

Projects in Bengkulu

Although colonization settlements were established in Bengkulu as far back as 1909, comparatively few migrants were settled in the area. The same has been true of transmigration undertakings since 1950. The main reason has been the comparative inaccessibility of Bengkulu, a factor responsible for the general underdevelopment of the whole province, which was part of South Sumatra until 1968. It is only since the commencement of the First Five-Year Development Plan in 1969 that serious attention has been given to regional planning and development in Bengkulu. In 1971 Bengkulu had only 519 366 people, with a density of 25 to the sq km. The mountainous terrain of the province, which has a very narrow coastal plain covered in swamps in many places, explains its low population density. Comparatively few independent migrants have been attracted to the province; communications with Java by sea are limited by the heavy seas on the west coast of southern Sumatra and the road linking the uplands of Bengkulu with Palembang in South Sumatra has never been in good condition.

In 1951 the Indonesian transmigration authority began sending migrants under *transmigrasi keluarga* to land available in former colonization villages. This policy was continued until 1958, during which period 1 952 people were settled in the Kemumu area; all the older Kemumu villages were transferred to the local government (in this instance the *marga* authorities) before 1962. A completely new project was established at Pekik Nyaring for general transmigrants in 1956–7.

In the period between 1963 and 1969, 6 071 migrants, many of them victims of the Mt. Agung eruption in Bali, were settled in five new projects (eleven villages) in different parts of Bengkulu. Of these, 3 564 have abandoned their holdings, most leaving in 1968 and 1969. A major reason for this has been trouble over land, which in many cases was not free from claims by local people. Many migrants also felt that there was little hope for the future development of these projects. On the whole economic growth has been hindered by the fact that settlements were too small for economic viability in terms of both size and number of settlers. Lack of roads and irrigation facilities was a further disadvantage. Only the seven new villages established in the Kemumu area and known collectively as the new Kemumu project have progressed at all. These villages had the advantage of good soil in a swamp-free area; access to markets enabled farmers to sell their products, though it is only since 1972, when the road linking Kemumu and Bengkulu was improved, that marketing has been easy. These seven settlements, however, are very small, having only 1 360 hectares of land and 2 932 settlers at the beginning of 1975, when plans were being made for transfer to the provincial government.

Of the other four projects established in the same period, none has really prospered. Apart from problems over land claimed by local people, the major problem has been the bad selection of sites. Settlements were often made in areas remote from population centres and far from the few existing roads, which made marketing of products virtually impossible. A further problem in many projects has been drainage. When the Pekik Nyaring project was established in 1956–7 with 2 104 settlers, drainage channels were constructed but they have proved inadequate, for the land intended for rice cultivation is under water for most of the year. In 1963 another 122 families were sent to the project but of these only six families remain. Those who have stayed in the project earn a living by selling timber and charcoal and making simple furniture for sale in Bengkulu, near which the project is situated. Another 1 918 migrants were settled in Pekik Nyaring in 1972–3 but nothing has yet been done about the problem of drainage.

The same is true of Talang Boseng, established early in 1969 with 952 settlers. In 1973–4, 1 617 *Banpres* migrants were placed at Talang Boseng. Very few of the original 1969 settlers remained at the end of 1974, when preparations were being made for trans-

fer of the project. The original location was very badly chosen, for it is several miles from the main road and bridges along the track leading to the project are in poor condition. Talang Boseng has the same problem as Pekik Nyaring in that land intended for rice fields cannot be used until the extensive swamps are properly drained. Settlers have fallen back on non-irrigated crops like cassava and the cultivation of coconuts. Another pre-1969 project, Kuro Tidur, which was set up in 1968, had to be abandoned completely; the migrants were shifted to other projects, because the site proved to be quite unsuitable.

In the first three years of the First Five-Year Plan, only one new project, Rimbo Kedui, was established in Bengkulu. It has not prospered, however, because of agricultural problems and distance (67 km) from the city of Bengkulu. Of the 469 people (100 families) settled there in 1971, only 265 people remain. It was intended that migrants should cultivate irrigated rice, using water from mountain streams. However, the swamps are too deep to be drained, and the area is completely under water, even in the dry season. Until a dam is constructed on the Air Seluma at Tais, thus allowing the swampy ground to drain naturally, the land cannot be used for agriculture.[20] Only home-lot crops like cassava and vegetables can be grown around houses; these are consumed by the migrants themselves. Even when there has been a surplus of such products, migrants have not been able to market them because bad roads and broken bridges make it impossible for them to transport anything out of the project area. For this same reason they cannot sell firewood, the commodity that in many instances in Bengkulu forms a good source of income for new settlers. To support themselves, some migrants work the fields of local people on a share-cropping basis. No migrants have been sent since the initial settlement was made in 1971; in 1975 the project is to be transferred to the local government.

The most successful of the recently established projects in Bengkulu is Bukit Peninjau-an. Situated on the main road only 23 km from Bengkulu, the provincial capital, the project has had no communication and marketing problems. Water is available throughout the year. Migrants are cultivating swamp rice and have themselves installed non-technical drainage, though there is obvious need for proper technical drainage. Rice yields so far have been low, averaging only 1 tonne per hectare, as a consequence of plagues of insects, which, as in other projects, have destroyed crops on newly cleared land. Cassava yields 30 tonnes per hectare, but migrants are being encouraged to grow rice since it will prove more profitable in the long run, for the province of Bengkulu still has to import rice from Java. Newcomers have succeeded in getting on well with local people and there have been no disputes over land. An extension known as Bukit Peninjauan II was made in 1974 to accommodate 400 families.

Between 1969 and March 1974, 6 135 migrants were settled in the Rimbo Kedui, Pekik Nyaring and Bukit Peninjauan projects. In addition, the Department of Social Welfare placed 1 568 migrants in four of its own projects for the unemployed and for victims of natural disasters. These projects have not done well and in 1974 it was decided to place the 867 people still living in Social Welfare projects under the care of the Directorate-General for Transmigration in the hope that more attention might be given to agricultural development.

A problem worth mentioning since it occurs in South Sulawesi is that of animals which destroy crops planted by migrants. This is somewhat different from the problem of wild pigs and rodents from forested areas. Hundreds of water-buffaloes roam freely in certain parts of Bengkulu, invading fields and trampling down crops. This has happened several times at Bukit Peninjauan, for example, forcing farmers to turn to the selling of firewood and charcoal to obtain additional income.[21] Nevertheless, the availability of water-buffaloes in the province has its good aspects, for it means that where irrigated farming is successfully established draught animals can be purchased by migrants or by the transmigration authority. The situation is quite different in Lampung where, even in the older settlements, there is a noticeable lack of draught animals.

The whole of Bengkulu receives a high annual rainfall that is reliable in both amount and distribution; numerous streams carry water down from the Bukit Barisan Ranges to the Indian Ocean throughout the year. This suggests that projects based on wet-rice cultivation could be established, provided that drainage is available, for the coastal plain to the north and south of the city of Bengkulu is very swampy. Meanwhile, it is essential that transmigration projects be incorporated into plans for provincial development, so as to avoid problems of the kind that arose in 1973. A change in plans for development of the capital of the Shire of North Bengkulu means a possible re-location of migrants in the Rama Agung project, which was established in 1963. Irrigation facilities of a simple nature have been constructed by settlers, who are cultivating rice on permanent fields. The provincial government has offered other land in compensation for the resumption of project land, but migrants are unwilling to move since the new land is still forested.[22] Unless a satisfactory solution is found, there may well be a repetition of the Gunung Balak problem in Lampung.

Projects in other Provinces of Sumatra

Jambi, to the north of South Sumatra, is the fourth province in the southern Sumatra region that is to receive priority in the settlement of migrants during the Second Five-Year Development Plan. Population density is low (16 persons to the sq km and only 0·84 per cent of Indonesia's total population in 1971), but much of the province consists of swamp-covered lowlands. In 1967 a small tidal project was established with 50 families in the Batanghari delta area on the island formed where the Berbak River, after branching from the Batanghari, flows into the Berhala Strait. Two larger settlements, established in the same place in 1969 and 1970 and known as Rantau Rasau I and Rantau Rasau II, did well enough to encourage further expansion of the project, and the original 4 000 hectares made available by the provincial government was increased to 18 000 hectares. By January 1975 there were six village units in the Rantau Rasau settlement area with a total population of 17 537, which includes some 3 000 local and completely independent settlers. A total of 7 236 hectares is now under cultivation and farmers are obtaining one crop of wet rice a year by means of tidally controlled irrigation. Primary canals have been constructed to enable water to flow from both the Batanghari and the Berbak through a network of channels similar to that in the Upang Delta. Secondary crops like corn, soya beans, peanuts and cassava are grown, along with fruit trees and coconut palms. In the 1974–5 wet season, *Bimas* was introduced on 263 hectares of irrigated rice fields in an attempt to test the extent to which present average yields of 1·5 tonnes per hectare of rice can be raised if fertilizer is used. The major problem of the Rantau Rasau villages is crop destruction by wild animals and insect pests. The fact that cultivated land is surrounded by heavy forest that encourages the breeding of insects makes spraying with insecticide comparatively ineffective. On the other hand, Rantau Rasau has no real marketing problems, easy communications and transportation being one of the assets of tidal projects. Small boats carry goods to and from the town of Jambi, which is the provincial capital. In a province that lacks an adequate road network, the rivers play a major role in communications. Meanwhile, plans have been made to settle migrants on non-tidal land in the western part of the province. Land has been made available in the vicinity of Sarolangun and Tanah Tembus, close to the Trans-Suma-

tra Highway. However, in the later years of the Second Five-Year Plan large tracts of tidal land are to be utilized for the establishment of more tidal-irrigation projects.

Three projects have been established in the Province of Riau, where population density is even lower (13 persons to the sq km). Of these, Siabu, established in 1962, has already been transferred to the provincial government while the others, Simandolak and Teluk Kiambang (which was established in 1972–3 and thus is not included in the projects listed in Table 7), are still under the care of the transmigration authority.

The Simandolak project, situated on 1 000 hectares close to the Kuantan River in the Upper Indragiri district, was established in 1969 as part of the Crash Program designed to accommodate migrants originally intended for settlement in tidal projects. In March 1972 there were 1 234 people in the project but no new migrants have been sent there since because the project has not been completely successful and economic development has been very slow. The reason can be traced to inadequate planning at the time of the hastily prepared Crash Program. The project was designed for ordinary farming but in fact the area is covered with seasonal swamps. In the wet season there is an excess of water while in the dry season there is often insufficient water for farming purposes. The migrants are not familiar with the techniques involved in the cultivation of swamp rice, a system that takes advantage of the seasonal fluctuations in the rivers and the floods that occur at certain times of the year, and neither guidance nor suitable farming equipment has been made available.[23] The dry land in the project area, intended for the cultivation of crops other than rice, has proved to be very infertile. Hence about one-third of the original migrants have left the settlement. As in other newly established projects, insect pests as well as wild pigs and rodents have attacked the crops. Rice yields have been extremely low (0·7 tonne per hectare in 1971 and 0·2 tonne in 1972)[24] and so settlers have been very much dependent on the supplies of food that the transmigration agency has been obliged to provide every month and on the cassava they grow in a few areas.

The Teluk Kiambang tidal project, also in the Province of Riau, was established in 1971–2 on 750 hectares of land on the southern bank of the estuary of the Indragiri River, and so far it has proved somewhat more successful than the Simandolak project. By March 1974, 1 472 migrants had been settled there and another 200 families will be placed there in 1974–5. Unfortunately, progress has been held up by land disputes; 52 hectares of land allocated to migrants was in fact owned by local people and so 17 families had to be resettled on another site.[25] Former dry fields, abandoned by shifting cultivators, have been converted to tidal rice fields covering 145 hectares and forest land has been cleared for dry fields, where corn and cassava are grown on 225 hectares. Marketing, however, is a major problem for the project is located too far from Tembilahan and the provincial capital of Pekanbaru for easy communications. There are no roads in the area and the river provides the only link with potential market centres. Malaria, too, has been a constant problem, as in other tidal projects.

The Province of West Sumatra (density 42 to the sq km) has received only limited attention from the transmigration authority in the years since 1969, despite the fact that 13 projects, with an initial settlement of 17 786 migrants, were established in this province between 1953 and 1968. One of the four projects set up in 1953, when for the first time the transmigration authority opened completely new projects, was made at Kapar, while in the same year more migrants were placed in a former Dutch colonization project at Batahan (also called Desa Baru). In 1954 a settlement was made at Tongar for Indonesians repatriated from Surinam but only 65 families (289 people) remained in 1974. Seven of the pre-1969 projects had already been

transferred to the provincial government by 1972, and another five (Kinali, Lepau Tempurung, Tongar, Dusun Tinggi and Tebing Tinggi, which together had 4 645 settlers in 1974) are to be transferred in 1975.

On the whole the projects in West Sumatra have not done well, mainly as the result of badly selected sites. The Dusun Tinggi project illustrates this problem. It was established in 1965 with 875 settlers but in 1974 only 328 people were still in the project area. The reason lies in the extremely isolated location of the settlement, which is in a small valley constantly threatened by floods. The soil, however, is fertile and it is this that has encouraged some of the original migrants to remain.[26] The project has not been able to prosper in the economic sense because farmers have difficulty in marketing the rice, corn and pulses that they grow. In terms of actual distance, the project is not far from roads and market centres, but the only link is a 7-km foot track that crosses two fast-flowing streams by way of narrow rope bridges. The irrigated land in the project could be extended but this is pointless as long as farmers are unable to market their produce.

The Sungai (usually abbreviated to Sei) Tambangan project, which, like Dusun Tinggi and Tebing Tinggi, is in the Shire of Sawahlunto, is better located from the point of view of proximity to roads and markets. The settlement was opened in 1965 on 2 610 hectares of land; in the 1965–8 period 507 families were settled there, but of these, only 287 families (1 391 people) remained in 1974. The project has not progressed so far as agriculture is concerned because migrants have found that they can earn a better living from sawmilling, since the surrounding land is well forested and there is a ready market for planks and beams. In 1973–4 another 772 migrants were sent to an extension of this project, while 1 339 people went to a completely new project opened at Lunang in the Shire of South Pesisir in the same year. The 2 111 people settled in these two projects

were the only migrants moved to West Sumatra between 1969 and 1974. However, in
1974–5 more people will go to Lunang and
Kinali, where the project originally established in 1966 is to be extended.

North Sumatra and Aceh, like Riau and
West Sumatra, are not included in the priority
provinces for transmigration during the Second Five-Year Plan. In the case of North Sumatra, the reason is that, with 94 persons to
the sq km, it is the most densely populated
province in Sumatra. Also, it is the province
with the highest percentage of plantations in
Indonesia. Hence there is little scope for settlements on the large scale now planned,
though there are many villages of Javanese migrants who were originally labourers on for-
eign-owned plantations in the pre-independ-
ence years.

In North Sumatra there have been only five
projects under the transmigration authority.
Of these, Bulungihit (1968) and Aek Naetek
(1973) are the most recent. The largest project is P.P.N. Baru (1960), which in March
1972 had 4 442 of the 7 721 people in the
existing projects. Many of the settlers in this
and the older projects, Merbabu (1959) and
Secanggang (1959), were former plantation
labourers who, after the nationalization of
Dutch estates in the late 1950s, settled on
land provided for this purpose.

Bulungihit, in the Shire of Labuhan Batu,
was first established with 200 families, plus
another nine local families, but in 1973 only
189 families (966 people) were left ·in the
project. The settlement has no irrigation and
rice, grown with natural rainfall, produces low
yields, the 1971 average being 1 tonne per hectare. The 1972 figure was only 0·4 tonne per
hectare, as a result of the long dry season and
insect pests.[27] Of the project area, 355·5 hectares are planted with rice, but unless irrigation facilities are provided, food will always
be a problem in the dry season, which in this
part of Sumatra is relatively long. In 1973–4 a
new project was established at Aek Naetek in
the same shire; 200 families (894 people)

were settled on 600 hectares and another 300
families will be placed in the same project
during 1974–5 to bring the number up to the
total of 500 families now considered to be the
optimum number of settlers for a village unit.
However, the fact that numbers of local people have been settling in this part of the province, after moving from North Tapanuli and
Tanah Karo,[28] seems to indicate that there is
not much scope for the establishment of new
projects. Migrants to be placed in North Sumatra during the first years of the Second
Five-Year Plan will go to a new project to be
established at Natal Batahan in the Shire of
South Tapanuli, where 20 000 hectares have
been made available for transmigration in a
district once considered by the Dutch government for a colonization settlement.[29]

In Aceh, the northernmost · province of
Sumatra, limited possibilities for farming do
not encourage the migration of farmers from
Java. Security disturbances in this province
during the 1950s were a further hindrance to
transmigration undertakings, while assimilation has not been easy because of local traditions. Added to this is the fact that distance
from Java makes the transportation of migrants difficult and expensive. Two settlements, involving only 1 186 people, were made
at Trumon (1963) and Blangpeute (1964),
very largely as a result of the policy of the time,
when it was considered desirable to have transmigration settlements in every province, irrespective of whether suitable land was available
and economic growth feasible. The failure of
the Blangpeute project did much to discredit
the whole concept of transmigration in the eyes
of the local people of the region,[30] and hence
no migrants were moved to Aceh during the
First Five-Year Plan. However, with the high
targets of the Second Plan, it has been decided to try to settle 2 500 families in this
province between 1974 and 1979. The locations chosen are in the Shire of Greater Aceh
for it is felt that if projects are close to the
capital of the province, supervision will be
easier. Furthermore, road communications in

this part of the province are reasonably good and thus marketing will be easy. The Department of Public Works will complete the Kreung Jreue irrigation project in 1975, while the Kreung Raya harbour is to be improved,[31] all of which will be to the advantage of transmigration settlements in the vicinity.

[1] *Rantjangan Dasar Undang-Undang Pembangunan Nasional-Semesta-Berentjana Delapan Tahun: 1961–1969*, op. cit., p. 2541.

[2] *Pelaksanaan Penempatan Transmigrasi Pelita I di Daerah Lampung*, Transmigration Directorate for Lampung (Tanjungkarang, 1973), p. 4.

[3] *Laporan Tahunan Direktorat Transmigrasi Propinsi Lampung Tahun Kerja 1973/1974* (Tanjungkarang, 1974), p. 5.

[4] *Transmigration Placement Viewed from the Irrigation Aspect*, Public Works Office, Province of Lampung (Telukbetung, 1973), p. 2.

[5] Widjojo Nitisastro, Minister of State for Economy, Finance and Industry, quoted in *Kompas* (2 August 1973), p. 1.

[6] *Laporan Tahunan Direktorat Transmigrasi Propinsi Lampung Tahun Kerja 1973/1974*, op. cit., p. 26.

[7] *Punggur Daerah Transmigrasi Dengan Pola Pertanian Sawah Beririgasi*, op. cit., p. 19.

[8] *Study Kasus Pada Proyek Transmigrasi Way Abung Dengan Pola Pertanian Tanah Kering*, Directorate-General for Transmigration (Jakarta, 1974), p. 40.

[9] One of the seven new irrigation projects planned for Lampung during the Second Five-Year Development Plan, 1974–1979. *Transmigration Placement Viewed from the Irrigation Aspect*, op. cit., p. 4.

[10] *Study Kasus Pada Proyek Transmigrasi Way Abung Dengan Pola Pertanian Tanah Kering*, op. cit., p. 25.

[11] Ibid., p. 34.

[12] Kampto Utomo, 'Masjarakat Transmigran Spontan Didaerah W. Sekampung (Lampung)', op. cit., p. 297.

[13] K.H. Junghans, 'Transmigration and Agricultural Production in Lampung' in *Transmigration in the Context of Area Development*, op. cit., p. 72.

[14] Amral Sjamsu, op. cit., p. 86.

[15] *Laporan Tahunan 1972–1973*, Transmigration Directorate for South Sumatra (Palembang, 1973), p. 5.

[16] *Program, Progress & Prospek*, op. cit., p. 15.

[17] *Ikhtisar Keadaan Proyek-Proyek Transmigrasi Propinsi Sumatera Selatan*, Transmigration Directorate for South Sumatra (Palembang, 1973), p. 8.

[18] *Perkembangan dan Pengembangan Produksi Daerah Pasang Surut Delta Upang*, Transmigration Directorate for South Sumatra (Palembang, 1974), p. 7.

[19] Ibid., p. 15.

[20] Irwaty, 'Transmigrasi dan Masalahnya di Propinsi Bengkulu', *Kompas* (16 Jan. 1974), p. 8.

[21] *Laporan Peninjauan Proyek Transmigrasi Propinsi Bengkulu Untuk Persiapan Penempatan Transmigrasi Tahun 1973–1974*, Directorate-General for Transmigration (Jakarta, 1973), p. 5.

[22] Ibid., p. 3.

[23] *Laporan Evaluasi Ekonomi, 1969 s/d 1972*, Transmigration Directorate for Riau (Pekanbaru, 1973), p. 6.

[24] Ibid., Table 5, p. 17.

[25] *Laporan Tahunan, Tahun ke-3*, op. cit., pp. 12 and 14.

[26] *Laporan Survey Evaluasi Proyek-Proyek Transmigrasi Sei Tambangan dan Dusun Tinggi, Sawahlunto, Sumatera Barat*, Directorate-General for Transmigration (Jakarta, 1972), p. 23.

[27] *Laporan Tahunan, Sumatera Utara, 1972/73*, Transmigration Directorate for North Sumatra (Medan, 1973), p. 1.

[28] Ibid., p. 4.

[29] Amral Sjamsu, op. cit., p. 59.

[30] 'Proyek Penempatan Transmigrasi Daerah Istimewa Aceh', in *Project Statement Program Pembangunan Transmigrasi Pelita II*, Buku II, Directorate-General for Transmigration (Jakarta, 1974), (no page numbers).

[31] *Rencana Pembangunan Lima Tahun Kedua 1974/75–1978/79*, IV, op. cit., p. 26.

VI

Projects Elsewhere in Indonesia

ALTHOUGH most of the migrants moved to transmigration settlements in the years since independence have gone to the southern provinces of Sumatra, as Table 7 indicates, projects have also been established in other islands of the archipelago with varying degrees of success. Large tracts of unused land are available for settlements but in many cases the very factors that have hindered economic development have likewise proved to be obstacles to the successful establishment of transmigration projects.

Kalimantan

A limiting factor in all development in Kalimantan is the extensive zone of swamps found along the southern and western coasts of the island. The eastern part of the island, however, is free from swamps and so attempts to resettle migrants from Java have tended to focus on this region. The whole of the Indonesian part of the island has a density of only 9 persons to the sq km (1971 census), with the highest concentration in the Province of South Kalimantan (49 to the sq km) where the cultivation of irrigated rice has long been practised in the Hulu Sungai district, and where population has increased accordingly, by comparison with areas where shifting agriculture is still found.

In the years between 1953 and 1968, almost 42 000 people were placed in projects throughout Kalimantan, while another 26 582 were settled there during the First Five-Year Development Plan (1969–1974). Of those moved between 1969 and 1974, 13 045 were placed in tidal-irrigation projects in West, Central and South Kalimantan. Kalimantan is one of the three priority regions selected for transmigration during the Second Five-Year Plan (Presidential Decree No. 2, 1973). More tidal

Table 12

Migrants Settled in Kalimantan and Sulawesi by Province, 1969–1974

Province	1969–70	1970–1	1971–2	1972–3	1973–4	Total
Kalimantan:						
East	961	1 806	814	1 804	3 955	9 340
South	631	729	1 877	1 448	2 327	7 012
Central	490	496	1 364	2 708	751	5 809
West	517	939	693	1 267	1 005	4 421
	2 599	3 970	4 748	7 227	8 038	26 582
Sulawesi:						
South	3 397	2 388	853	3 953	9 511	20 102
South-east	–	1 004	1 924	2 875	3 208	9 011
Central	740	3 764	2 343	4 564	3 663	15 074
North	–	286	–	552	2 667	3 505
	4 137	7 442	5 120	11 944	19 049	47 692

Source: Directorate-General for Transmigration (Jakarta, April 1974).

Table 13
Migrants Settled in Kalimantan by Project, 1969–1974

Project	1969–70	1970–1	1971–2	1972–3	1973–4	Total
Maluku	961	62			359	1 382
Lempake		754	449	280	380	1 863
Sukarame		107				107
Samboja		382	365			747
Pulau Atas		455		174	1 441	2 070
Long Iram		46				46
Manggar				211		211
Bukit Biru				993		993
Palaran				146	1 273	1 419
Purwajaya					502	502
Barambai	631	729	1 877	1 034		4 271
Tambarangan				414	2 327	2 741
Tamban Luar	490	496	1 146	2 708		4 840
Mentaren			218		751	969
Parit Strabidi	517					517
Kubu II		939				939
Sei Rasau			693	1 267	1 005	2 965
	2 599	3 970	4 748	7 227	8 038	26 582

Source: Directorate-General for Transmigration, Jakarta, April 1974.

projects will be opened in West and Central Kalimantan, while in the eastern part of the island attention will be given to the establishment of dry-farming projects close to the highway now under construction between Banjarmasin, Balikpapan and Samarinda.

The Province of East Kalimantan

In the years between 1954 and March 1974, 26 projects of varying sizes were established in East Kalimantan (density 4 persons to the sq km in 1971). Of these, only five had been transferred by the end of the First Five-Year Plan; the remainder are to be handed over to the local provincial government during 1975. On the whole, the projects established in this province before 1969 have not prospered. As in other regions, the reasons can be traced to bad selection of sites, poor soils, inadequate preparation of project land before settlement was commenced and, in some cases, lack of markets for agricultural products. In the case of East Kalimantan, one further factor is that in many instances political motives were involved in the selection of settlers and the choice of sites. In 1954 and 1955 political detainees from West Java (283 families) were sent to the Samboja projects. Later, in the 1960s, when larger numbers of people were settled outside Java as a consequence of the National Transmigration Movement, East Kalimantan was again selected for settlements. In the 1962–5 period alone, approximately 9 500 people were moved to East Kalimantan where 'for political reasons in the Dwikora confrontation period, transmigration projects were located close to the border and far from markets'.[1] As a result of the inevitable economic stagnation in these and other transmigration projects in the province, relatively large numbers of migrants have left project areas to seek employment in urban districts or with timber companies. Many of those who have remained in settlements have earned a living from the gathering of wood and other forest products rather than from agriculture.

Of the projects established before 1969, the most successful have been the Palaran and Bukuan settlements, which have expanded economically because of fairly good soil and proximity to Samarinda. With the cultivation of rice by Javanese settlers, the shortages experienced in Samarinda have been less acute. Migrants have found it easy to transport all their products, which include baskets, mats, household utensils and similar handicraft products, to market by boat, for these projects are located close to the Mahakam River, not too far upstream from the mouth. Although the lack of technical irrigation means that only one crop of rice can be grown annually, migrants have found that there is a demand in Samarinda for dry-season crops like corn.

On the other hand, the Loah Janan project to the south of Samarinda and the Baturatna project to the north of Balikpapan have done less well, largely because of hilly land and poor soil. Also, many of the migrants originally settled in the latter project were moved by the Department of Social Welfare, and they have been described as 'lazy and lacking in perseverance'.[2] In general it is true that those people moved because of natural disasters or because they could not find employment in the urban areas of Java tend to be lacking in initiative and enthusiasm, and sometimes in farming skills. At the same time it must be admitted that the sites selected for such people have often been quite unsuitable for agriculture.

The least successful projects have been the nine small ones located in the vicinity of Long Iram in the Hulu Mahakam area, many miles upstream from Samarinda. The twelve villages in these projects were established in 1964 and 1965, when political concepts about 'filling the empty spaces' took priority over economic considerations in the selection of sites. A glance at the figures given in Table 14 for Lenggang Amir and the eight projects immediately following reveals a further reason, apart from isolation, for the lack of economic progress. Settlers were given only 1 hectare of land per family and the number of families placed in each project was very small. Experience has shown that settlements must be close enough to each other and of sufficient size to warrant the input of infrastructure and facilities necessary for economic expansion. Despite their lack of development, these nine projects are to be transferred to the provincial government in 1975, and land titles have already been given to 563 families in five of the projects where claims to project land by other people have already been settled.[3]

In the 1954–68 period approximately 19 000 migrants were settled in East Kalimantan, while another 9 340 people were moved to the province between 1969 and 1974 by the Directorate-General for Transmigration. Of those moved in the second period, 5 083 were 'sectoral' migrants, for whom a large percentage of the necessary finance was provided by provincial governments (either the provincial government of East Kalimantan or provincial governments in Java); the migrants were, however, placed in projects under the care and responsibility of the transmigration authority. To accommodate these migrants, six new projects were opened (see Table 13) but migrants were also sent to the older projects of Samboja, Pulau Atas, Palaran and Long Iram.

During the First Five-Year Plan, the Directorate-General for Natural Disasters moved another 2 713 people to East Kalimantan, placing them in both ordinary transmigration projects and special Department of Social Welfare projects. In some cases they were settled in projects already transferred to the provincial government; for example, 308 people who had lost their homes and fields as a result of *lahar* (mud flows) from Mt. Merapi in 1973 were resettled in the former Petung project.[4]

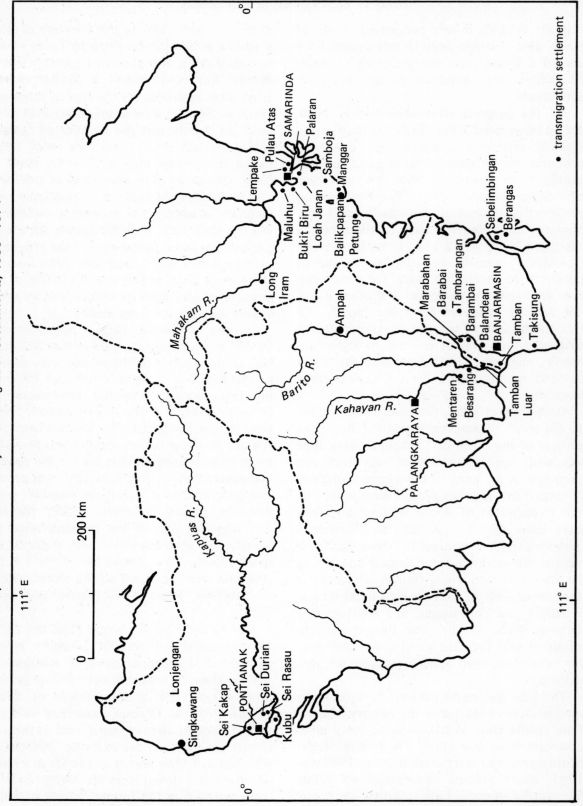

70

Map 5: Kalimantan: major transmigration settlements, 1950–1974

● transmigration settlement

111° E

111° E

0°

0°

SAMARINDA

Palaran

Pulau Atas

Lempake

Samboja

Manggar

Balikpapan

Petung

Maluhu

Bukit Biru

Loah Janan

Sebelimbingan

Berangas

Long Iram

Marabahan

Tambarangan

Barabai

BANJARMASIN

Barambai

Balandean

Tamban

Takisung

Ampah

Mahakam R.

Barito R.

Kahayan R.

PALANGKARAYA

Mentaren

Besarang

Tamban Luar

Kapuas R.

200 km

0

Lonjengan

Singkawang

Sei Kakap

PONTIANAK

Sei Durian

Kubu

Sei Rasau

Table 14
Transmigration Projects in East Kalimantan, 1954–1968

Project	Years of settlement	Original project area (ha)	Number of migrants[1]	Year of transfer
1. Palaran	1954–64	10 000	2 375	1965
2. Petung	1954–64	5 250	2 673	1971
3. Waru	1959–64	7 800	1 516	1971
4. Bukuan	1962–3	10 000	864	1965
5. Baturatna	1962–5	3 500	2 679	1971
6. Samboja	1954	1 000	1 231	
7. Loah Janan	1961–4	3 000	986	
8. Pulau Atas	1957	1 000	1 938	
9. Lenggang Amir	1964	340	417	
10. Lenggang Bigung	1964	342	497	
11. Sekolaq Darat	1964	270	481	
12. Sekolaq Jolek	1964–5	456	844	
13. Long Iram	1965	290	663	
14. Tering	1965	175	293	
15. Mencimai	1965	160	312	
16. Empas	1965	530	951	
17. Barong Tongkok	1965	80	139	

Source: Compiled from data in *Laporan Tahunan Tahun ke-3, Pelita I, 1971/1972*, op. cit., Enclosure IV, and *Laporan Kegiatan Direktorat Transmigrasi Propinsi Kalimantan Timur Tahun I s/d IV Pelita* (Samarinda, 1973), p. 5 (a) and (b).

Note: [1] These figures refer to the number of migrants placed in projects between the years stated as years of settlement and not to the number still living in projects.

A major reason for the limited success of some of the larger East Kalimantan projects, apart from unsuitable geographical conditions, has been the fact that frequently more than one agency has been involved in settlement work. Many of the projects have been set up in conjunction with the Department of Social Welfare while others have been established in co-operation with the provincial government, which has always shown interest in having more people settle in East Kalimantan. However, lack of co-ordination between the different agencies has often meant inadequate preparation of project sites and insufficient guidance of migrants after arrival. Since the ratification of the 1972 Basic Transmigration Act, with its stipulation that the transmigration agency is responsible for the establish-

ment and care of projects, co-ordination has been better.

In so far as most migrants who have left the various projects have remained in the province, one of the aims of transmigration—the provision of labour for development of natural resources—is being attained. East Kalimantan has large forest reserves and since 1968 forestry concessions have been given to both domestic and foreign logging companies. Unlike migrants in other provinces where agricultural settlements have, for one reason or another, not provided a good living, migrants who have left projects in East Kalimantan have easily found employment in the logging industry and in harbour areas from which timber is exported. So far, nothing has been done about linking transmigration with the forestry industry. In cases where the Department of Manpower (since April 1973, combined with Transmigration and Co-operatives in one department) has organized and supervised the employment of labourers from Java in logging companies, the movement of workers has been on a contract basis and they have had the option of returning to Java at the end of the period of contract. Meanwhile, the transmigration agency has encountered problems with forestry companies holding exploitation rights to areas selected for transmigration settlements in East Kalimantan. Since relatively large numbers of migrants are to be settled in this province during the Second Five-Year Plan, it is essential that these problems be solved in the very near future.

The Province of South Kalimantan

South Kalimantan has the highest population density in Kalimantan but by comparison with any province in Java it is very much underpopulated. Since the population tends to be concentrated along the Barito River and close to the road linking Banjarmasin with Tanjung, an attempt was made in the 1950s and 1960s to locate transmigration projects in the more sparsely populated parts of the province. On the whole, however, the projects established before 1969 have not prospered, the major reasons being poor soils in the areas selected and bad communications.

The first project was opened at Takisung in 1953. In 1957 a tidal-irrigation project was commenced at Tamban, followed by two more tidal projects at Marabahan (1959) and Balandean (1961); 10 355 people were settled in the four projects, which have already been transferred to the provincial government, despite their slow economic progress. Large numbers of migrants have left these and the other projects established in the early 1960s (Berangas in 1960 and Sebelimbingan in 1961) and have found work as labourers in Banjarmasin, where there are several saw mills. Berangas and Sebelimbingan, both dry-farming projects on the island of Pulau Laut off the south-east

coast of South Kalimantan, have not done well because of poor soils. Of the 1 745 people originally settled in the two projects, only 1 106 (276 families) remained in 1974, when preparations were being made to issue land-ownership certificates for the 798 hectares under cultivation, in readiness for transfer to the provincial government in 1975.[5] Two other projects, Bantuil and Danau Salak, which were opened by the provincial government in conjunction with other agencies, have progressed no better than the six set up by the transmigration agency in the pre-1969 period.

During the First Five-Year Plan, the Directorate-General for Transmigration settled 7 012 people in two new projects, one at Barambai (1969) and the other at Tambarangan (1973). The second of these, where 2 741 migrants were settled, is located in the Shire of Tapin, 118 km to the north-east of Banjarmasin. Despite its comparative proximity to the Banjarmasin-Tanjung road, communications still present problems because there are no paved roads linking the project with the main provincial road. Settlers are dependent upon dry farming but soils have proved to be poor, and fertilizers and even seed for planting are not easily obtainable. Despite these problems, most of the partly assisted and *Banpres* migrants who moved to South Kalimantan in 1973 and 1974 have been settled in the same area, where large tracts of land free from claims by local people are available. In addition to the 1 692 migrants who moved under the *Banpres* programme in March and April 1974, another 5 136 people moved to South Kalimantan as completely independent migrants during the First Five-Year Plan, settling for the most part in the Shire of Tapin, though 1 051 chose to go to older projects like Takisung and Tamban.

South Kalimantan differs significantly from East Kalimantan in that there are large areas of swamp land and also land that is flooded seasonally. Many years ago, the local people living around Banjarmasin devised ways of making use of certain parts of the swamp lands for the cultivation of rice. Farmers learned to take advantage of the tidal influence that extends as far as 100 km inland in the larger rivers and their tributaries. The techniques they perfected by trial and error over the years were later introduced into eastern Sumatra.

Not all parts of coastal Kalimantan are suitable for tidal irrigation. The site chosen must be close enough to the coast for tidal effects to be felt daily but not so close that crops are affected by the salt water that penetrates some miles inland in the dry season. At the same time, the location must be such that annual floods in the wet season are not too extensive. In some places farmers construct large dykes or embankments along primary canals to prevent the complete inundation of their fields. Obviously a thorough knowledge of the local river regime is necessary before a site can be chosen for tidal rice fields.

Only a certain type of rice can be grown in tidal areas. The average growth period of eleven months is relatively long, a reflection of the nature of soils in swamp areas, where acidity is high. In southern Kalimantan farmers first cultivate the seeds in a seed-bed during October; the young plants are transplanted two or even three times before being transferred to the field in March, when there is less danger of flooding. Six months later, in August or September, before the heavy rains of the next wet season begin, the crop is ready for harvest. Farmers in tidal areas face the usual problem of insect pests and animals like wild pigs and rodents, which commonly appear when fields are situated in forest areas.

From the point of view of transmigration, the establishment of projects in tidal areas offers certain attractions, one being that such regions are sparsely populated and so land can be obtained fairly easily. Also there is no clash of interests with forestry undertakings. Experiences in the Barambai project, however, have indicated once again the need for proper land records in all parts of the coun-

try. Of the 5 752 hectares made available by the provincial government for transmigration, much was already being cultivated by local people, many of whom were shifting cultivators with no clear title to the land under cultivation. Settlement work was delayed at first until land problems were brought to a satisfactory conclusion with the payment of compensation for land along the major canals to be constructed in the project area and for crops growing on such land. Even where land titles existed, boundaries between holdings were not clearly defined. It was decided that the 373 local families (1 992 people) should remain within the project area. Fortunately relations between migrants and local people have been extremely good; one advantage in Kalimantan as far as transmigration is concerned is that the assimilation of newcomers presents no problems, no doubt because various different groups of people have settled in this region over the centuries.

Between 1969 and 1973, 4 271 migrants were settled at Barambai under General Transmigration. With the arrival of some independent migrants in 1973–4, the population was 4 741 in March 1974. A total of 1 964 hectares was under cultivation, 1 718·5 hectares being wet rice fields and the remainder home gardens. Those migrants who settled before 1973 have already been given land certificates in order to avoid any confusion over land rights when the project is transferred in 1975.

Another major attraction in tidal areas lies in the fact that it is much cheaper to settle migrants in such districts than on land that has to be irrigated in the normal way. The construction of dams is avoided, as is the construction of roads, for canals and rivers function as a means of communication. By comparison with dry-farming projects, however, the tidal projects may turn out in the long run to be much more expensive.

The essential thing in the planning of tidal projects is a careful selection of sites. A survey made of the Barambai project in 1972, almost three years after settlement began, found that in fact fresh water from the Barito does not reach the rice fields because the tidal influence at that point does not carry the water far enough.[6] The Barambai project, unlike the Upang Delta project, is laid out on a fork pattern. The primary canal runs westwards from the Barito for 1·4 km and then branches, with a secondary canal to the left and another to the right. The tidal influence extends only 1·5 km from the Barito. In principle fresh water should be carried to the tertiary channels and thence to the fields, and with drainage of water from the fields acidity should be reduced. However, the opposite is happening, because there is no exchange of water. Thus acidity is in fact increasing, because the influence of the swamp water more than counterbalances the effect of the fresh water. In the dry season it has been found that the water level of the Barito at this point drops by a metre or so, and hence the water cannot reach the fields. The situation could possibly be helped by the installation of a pumping unit to lift river water. The same report also pointed out that canals and channels are becoming shallow as a consequence of sedimentation, while weed growth is further obstructing them.[7] Obviously if canals are to function as a means of communication also, they must be deep enough to allow the passage of small motor-boats.

One feature of the system used in this and certain other tidal projects in Kalimantan is that the same channels are used for both the supply of water and drainage. A kind of pool or tank is made at the end of the secondary canals to make possible the replacement of water. The system works less effectively, however, than the system of double channels used in the Upang Delta project, because swamp water tends to flow into the fresh water.

Perhaps the real criterion by which the tidal projects both in Kalimantan and in eastern Sumatra should be judged is that of soil fertility. A fact that was overlooked in some of the earlier tidal projects is that the indigenous people of these areas have always been essentially shifting cultivators, for this kind of swamp cultivation has implied a move to new land every few years, and hence cultivation techniques have been very simple. Like the shifting cultivator growing dry rice in forest clearings, the cultivator in tidal areas has not depended exclusively on his rice crop for his livelihood. He has always been able to sell timber, firewood and other forest products like rattan, collected in the vicinity. The very fact that much of the Barambai area was already planted with rubber, for which compensation had to be paid by the transmigration authority, indicates that in fact the local people had converted former fields to rubber gardens, albeit of poor quality, when soil fertility began to decrease.

That this last aspect is an important consideration has already been shown by the failure of the Marabahan project (1959), approximately 17 km further upstream from Barambai on the Barito River. In less than ten years the fields were covered in scrub and weeds, although the water channels had been well designed and constructed. The problem here has been a decrease in soil fertility as a consequence of cultivation on the same land in successive years, to the point where now nothing can be grown.[8] Migrants have left the project area to find employment elsewhere.

For that reason, it is essential that those who settle in tidal projects be given more than 2 hectares of land in order to allow some flexibility in the use of fields. In a region with conventional irrigation, a farmer, assisted only by his family, may be unable to cultivate 2 hectares in an intensive fashion. But the tidal projects are much more correctly in the same category as the dry-farming projects, where 2 hectares are certainly not enough. It is for that reason that the new policy of allowing extra land is now being applied in tidal areas, even though the same concept of mixed farming is certainly not envisaged.

Another aspect that hindered the development of tidal projects in the past was the fact that frequently the necessary infrastructure of canals and channels was not ready when migrants began to arrive. This technical work has been the task of the Project for Opening Tidal Rice-Land, which comes under the Department of Public Works. Since design and preparation have demanded considerable survey work in advance, it has often happened that implementation has lagged behind transmigration plans for the transportation and settlement of migrants, as has happened in other areas like Lampung where conventional irrigation facilities were planned. But whereas the migrant in dry-land areas can at least start planting cassava, the migrant placed in a tidal area can do very little, added to which is his complete lack of familiarity with a tidal environment. Related to this is the fact that the timing of the arrival of migrants is particularly important in tidal areas, although this too is a consideration in all settlements. Migrants should arrive in the Kalimantan projects in July so that they can begin preparing fields for the approaching wet season. Land has to be cleared of tree and plant growth and seeds have to be sown in seed-beds before the heavy rains of the west monsoon begin.

It is now realized that some form of training is necessary before migrants are sent to tidal projects. Farmers from Java, Madura and Bali alike have had no experience of tidal cultivation techniques, and in the past have found it difficult to adapt to the new pattern of farming required in these areas. The inability of settlers to adjust to the different environment has been one of the reasons for the slow growth of these projects. More attention is now being given to this, and also to the health aspect. The Barambai project has a polyclinic which is frequented by local people who, before the establishment of the project, had extremely limited health and educational facilities. Malaria remains a major complaint, while the lack of adequate supplies of drinking water gives rise to other sicknesses.

The Province of Central Kalimantan

Only four transmigration projects have been established in this province, which is probably the least developed part of Kalimantan and, like East Kalimantan, has a population density of only 4 persons to the sq km. However, it lacks the petroleum resources of the latter province and has no towns comparable to Balikpapan and Samarinda in size. The swamp zone in the southern part of the province has proved to be a hindrance to agricultural development and to communications, though several companies have begun logging operations further inland, making use of the large rivers of the province to float logs downstream to the estuaries.

The first major transmigration project in Central Kalimantan was established in 1960 at Mentaren, on the eastern bank of the Kahayan River. Progress has been slow, but more migrants were sent there in 1971–2 in an attempt to stimulate growth. Besarang (1961) has likewise been slow to expand. Both of these projects were planned on the polder system, which involves the construction of dykes to prevent flooding and of canals for drainage purposes. A third project at Pematang Tujuh has remained small. The largest settlement in the province is that at Tamban Luar, established in 1969 when transmigration policies favoured tidal projects. During the First Five-Year Plan, 4 840 migrants were settled in this project.

The Tamban Luar project is located close to the point where the Anjir Tamban, a canal linking the lower Kapuas River with the Barito and parallel to the Anjir Serapat, meets the Kapuas. It lies in the Pulau Petak Delta, where tidal influence is found as far as 80 km inland. This whole delta area has been formed in a manner which is typical of lowland Kalimantan. Several miles upstream from Banjarmasin, the Barito branches. The western branch, the Murung, flows south-west to join the Kapuas. The boundary between South and Central Kalimantan passes through this triangular-shaped delta region. Most of the tidal projects of the two provinces are located in this area, which is the major unit in the work being

Map 6:   The Tamban Luar Settlement: sketch of canal network

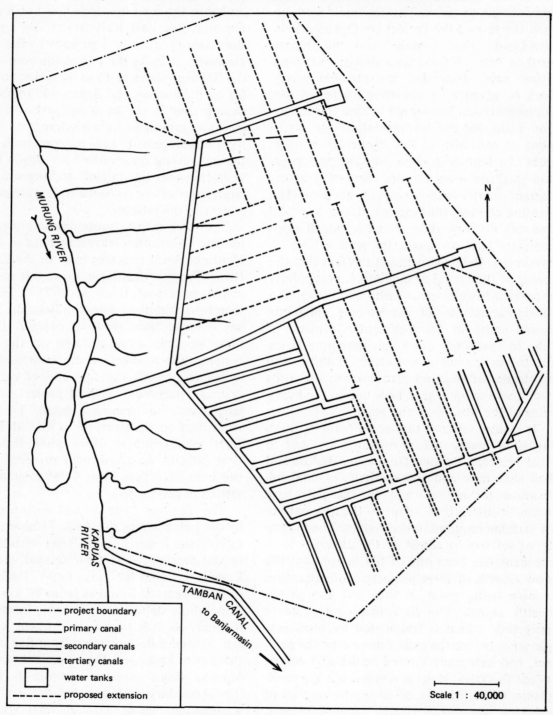

Source: *Laporan Survey Checking Explorasi Persiapan*
Perluasan Penempatan Proyek Trans. Tamban Luar,
Kalimantan Tengah (Jakarta, 1972).

done in southern Kalimantan by the Project for Opening Tidal Rice-land.[9]

The Tamban Luar settlement has an area of 3 500 hectares. The system of water control used in the Barambai project has also been used here, though with better results, since there is no difficulty in obtaining fresh water from the river. Tidal influences at the point where the project is located lift the water level by more than 1 metre, even in the dry season, and at high tide the effect extends for more than 2 km from the bank of the Kapuas.[10] The primary canal, like that at Barambai, runs straight from the river for 2 km, then branches to left and right with a third canal continuing towards the east. At high tide river water can reach the tanks, which are located about 6 or 7 km from the point where the secondary canals branch from the primary. As in other tidal projects, rice with a very long growing period is cultivated. The Tamban Luar project has had the advantage of having no land problems, since the land allocated for transmigration purposes was quite clearly state land and there were no local shifting cultivators in the vicinity.

Distance from markets will continue to be a major hindrance to the economic growth of projects in this part of Kalimantan. Palangkaraya, the provincial capital, is an administrative rather than a commercial centre, and as yet the province has no major port. Goods are transported from Tamban Luar via the Tamban Canal to Banjarmasin, a distance of 38 km (6 to 7 hours by boat). This and the other canals, however, like the rivers of the area, require constant dredging to keep them deep enough for navigation; in recent years this has been somewhat neglected. However, despite problems of communications, the fact that population density is very low and large tracts of land, free from any claims, are available means that Central Kalimantan will certainly be able to provide more locations for transmigration settlements during the course of the Second Five-Year Development Plan.

The Province of West Kalimantan

Several transmigration projects have been established in West Kalimantan but on the whole they have not progressed very rapidly. Originally this province was not included in those receiving priority in the settlement of migrants during the Second Five-Year Plan, but with improved security in the border district to the north of Pontianak and the obvious need for more sedentary farmers in the province (population density 13 to the sq km), it was decided to make West Kalimantan the eleventh province to receive large numbers of settlers (Presidential Decree No. 12, 1973).

In the 1955–68 period eight settlements were made, during which time 6 531 migrants were moved to the province. Of these, only two (Kubu I and Sei Durian) had been transferred to the provincial government by 1974. The main reasons for the slow development of these older projects can be traced to the lack of good seed, fertilizer and insecticide, to poor drainage and, in dry areas, to inadequate supplies of water. Communications have also been a problem, for there are very few roads in the province. The Kelang project (1970), for example, needs better drainage channels, as well as a road to link it with the town of Kubu, 7 km away, and at least one motor-boat to transport agricultural products from the project to Pontianak.

Most of the 4 421 migrants who moved to West Kalimantan between 1969 and 1974 went to Sei (Sungai) Rasau, a tidal project located in the delta of the Kapuas River,[11] where the Department of Public Works has estimated that 7 500 hectares could be used for tidal-irrigation farming. Situated on the Rasau River, which flows into the Punggur Besar River, itself a tributary of the Kapuas, the Sei Rasau project covers more than 1 000 hectares and is the centre from which more tidal settlements are to be established. The project has been successful agriculturally since the water channels have been well designed and so function efficiently. However, the marketing of produce is a problem. A road linking Sei

Table 15
Migrants Settled in Sulawesi by Project, 1969–1974

Project	1969–70	1970–1	1971–2	1972–3	1973–4	Total
Bone-Bone	2 253	1 961	853		5 249	10.316
Mangkutana	1 144	427		3 953	1 329	6 853
Wotu					1 481	1 481
Masamba					1 452	1 452
Landono		378	1 924	442		2 744
Mowila				517		517
Rambu-Rambu		626				626
Ladongi				1 916	3 208	5 124
Parigi	740	3 764	2 343	1 692		8 539
Lembontonara				2 409		2 409
Rowa				463	244	707
Mepanga					2 019	2 019
Toili					1 400	1 400
Domuga		286				286
Tapadaka				552	1 943	2 495
Paguyaman					724	724
	4 137	7 442	5 120	11 944	19 049	47 692

Source: Directorate-General for Transmigration (Jakarta, April 1974).

Rasau with the much older project at Sei Durian, only 7 km away, would make the new project less isolated and would also help the marketing of products.

Migrants were also settled at Kubu II, an extension of an earlier project already transferred, and at Patok 20. In the first years of the Second Five-Year Plan migrants will go to Sei Rasau and Kelang, and also to Anjungan, a new project to be established in a non-tidal area. With the construction of new roads linking Pontianak with other major centres, such as Sinkawang and Sintang, possibilities will exist for the establishment of non-tidal projects in districts away from the coastal swamp zone.

Sulawesi

Sulawesi differs geographically from Sumatra and Kalimantan in several respects, two of the most important being the length of the dry season and the limited areas of flat land. There is a similarity, however, in the fact that soils on the whole are not very fertile. Population density for the whole island was 37 persons to the sq km in 1971. The three southern provinces together form the third of the regions to which greater numbers of migrants will be sent in the 1974–9 period.

As has been pointed out in an earlier chapter, several attempts had been made to establish colonization projects in Sulawesi during Dutch colonial times, and those in the Luwu area of South Sulawesi were beginning to prosper when the Second World War broke out. After independence, the Indonesian government considered the possibility of moving people to this island, but at that time the southern part of Sumatra offered greater attractions. However, the proximity of Sulawesi to East Java, Bali and Lombok is a great advantage from the point of view of transportation, while climatic conditions are not unlike those in East Java, where farmers are accustomed to a dry season of four to five months a year. Added to this is the further advantage that religious and cultural traditions in Sulawesi are such that newcomers are readily accepted.

The Province of South Sulawesi

It was only in 1969 that the Indonesian transmigration authority considered the possibility of placing migrants in the less populated parts of South Sulawesi. In 1951 and 1952 a total of 437 people had been sent under *transmigrasi keluarga* to join relatives living in former Dutch projects near Bone-Bone and Masamba in the Luwu area. However, the disturbances that disrupted the economic as well as the political stability of the southern part of Sulawesi for most of the 1950s and the early years of the 1960s forced the government to look to the northern peninsula for settlement sites.

When a Crash Program was drawn up at the beginning of the First Five-Year Plan, for migrants originally to be settled in tidal areas, the Shire of Luwu was chosen as one of the project sites, one of the major reasons for the choice being the availability of large tracts of land free from any claims. The system of communally owned land, held under *adat* or traditional law, which has proved a great handicap to the procurement of suitable project land in much of Sumatra, is not found in Sulawesi, where disputes with local people over land have been very few. Furthermore, a survey of the area, made at approximately the same time as the first settlement, indicated that the alluvial plain that makes up much of the Shire of Luwu offered good possibilities for agricultural development.[12]

Added to these considerations was the fact that the provincial government of South Sulawesi showed great interest in having more people settle in the northern part of the province. Although the population density for the whole province was 63 to the sq km in 1971,

the figure for the Shire of Luwu was slightly less than 10 to the sq km.

Between 1969 and 1974, 20 102 people were settled in Luwu. Most of them were fully sponsored (*umum*) migrants, in accordance with the government's policy of placing such migrants in newly established projects and of sending partly assisted migrants to areas where prosperous settlements already exist. The migrants sent to Luwu have received the normal allowances in the form of free transportation, farming tools, seed, housing, kitchen utensils, clothing and bedding and basic foodstuffs for their first twelve months in the new settlements, as well as the 2 hectares of land given to all migrants. In 1973–4, partly sponsored migrants who received only limited assistance with transportation were settled in some of the 1969–70 villages.

Progress in the Luwu settlements has been comparatively rapid, but certain major problems, by no means limited to the transmigration villages, have hindered further economic expansion. The most significant of these is marketing of agricultural produce. Migrants have no incentive to produce more than they can consume or to cultivate commercial crops, because of the difficulty they have in selling products. In the case of Luwu, however, the problem is not identical with that faced in other parts of the country where projects have been established in remote areas. The difficulty in Luwu lies in the fact that the whole of the shire is virtually cut off from the rest of the province and from other parts of Sulawesi by the poor condition of the existing road network. Within the Shire of Luwu farmers have trouble in transporting products even as far as the shire capital of Palopo. During the political disturbances of earlier years, most of the bridges spanning the rivers that flow across the Luwu plain were destroyed and are only now being replaced or repaired.[13] Hence very few buses or trucks make the difficult 92-km journey from Palopo to the town of Bone-Bone.

Ultimately this problem of poor communi-

Map 7: Sulawesi: major transmigration settlements, 1950—1974

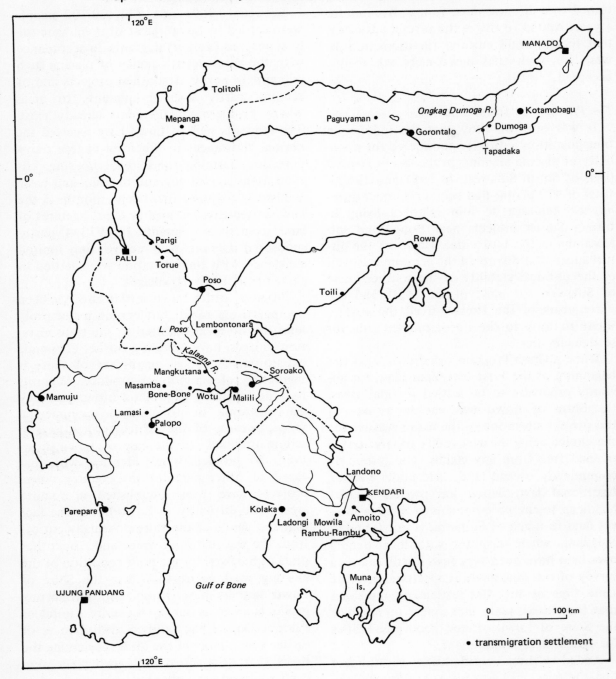

transmigration settlement

cations will be removed with the completion of the Trans-Sulawesi Highway, of which the existing road is to form a section. Most of the transmigration settlements lie fairly close to this highway, which will link North and Central Sulawesi with Ujung Pandang via the Shire of Luwu. Work intended to improve the small harbours around the northern section of the Gulf of Bone is already in progress; this will assist the transportation of migrants to the area and the removal of agricultural products.[14] For most of Sulawesi, the sea has for centuries provided the main trade routes and, since road construction in this mountainous island is expensive, the use of boats still continues to be significant.

In the Luwu area the mistake so often made in past years of locating small-scale settlements in remote areas, where an adequate infrastructure is never likely to be provided, has been avoided. The village unit concept, which is to guide village design and organization in coming years, has already been introduced in Luwu. By March 1974, there were four projects in the shire, with a total of 11 villages.

The first project established in Luwu was located close to the original Dutch settlement at Tamuku in the District of Bone-Bone; in October 1974, the seven village units in the project had a total population of 12 468 settlers. Conscious of the need to leave land for future expansion and thus avoid the fragmentation of holdings already apparent in southern Lampung, the Directorate-General for Transmigration established another project in the District of Mangkutana, in the vicinity of the Dutch settlement of Kalaena in the eastern part of the shire. The two villages established at Kertoraharjo had 3 223 settlers in October 1974; more migrants will be placed there in the early years of the Second Five-Year Plan. A third project, having as yet only one village unit, has been established in the Wotu District, while a fourth project, also with only one village unit, has been established in the Masamba District. These two

projects will be expanded as more settlers are moved into the area and new villages founded.

The lack of adequate irrigation facilities in most of the new settlements means that migrants can grow only one crop of rice a year, since they are forced to depend upon natural rainfall. The Department of Public Works has continued work on irrigation networks originally planned and partly constructed by the Dutch colonization authority. The canals draw water from the Kanjiro, Bone-Bone and Kalaena Rivers and, as construction work continues, more land will have full irrigation. Migrants have assisted with the work in some villages, receiving food from World Food Programme as payment for this and similar work that has included road construction and the repair of small bridges.

A major problem in the flatter parts of the Luwu plain is drainage. The rivers of the area are comparatively short and shallow but they tend to be broad; when heavy rain falls in the mountains that form the northern part of the shire, floods occur, making roads completely impassable and often inundating rice fields. Progress in one of the Bone-Bone villages has been completely obstructed by the fact that the site was badly chosen. Location close to a river was considered an advantage for village-style irrigation; the area, however, is subject to frequent floods. An embankment was constructed along the river bank to keep water off the fields and village, with the result that rice fields could not be drained. It was then decided to move the village to higher land and to abandon the fields. The Department of Public Works has now decided to construct a dam higher up the river; although this is a much more costly solution, it means that a comparatively large area of land, now only sparsely settled because of floods, will be available for migrants in a few years' time.

Certain problems have arisen in some of the newer settlements, particularly those in the Mangkutana area, because of lack of coordination between transmigration plans and those of the irrigation section within the Public Works Department. Migrants have been re-luctant to clear land and lay out dyked fields unless they feel confident that irrigation water will soon be available. The ideal ar-rangement is to have the two activities of canal construction and land preparation take place within the same co-ordinated plan. In view of experiences in the Way Seputih area of Lampung, settlers cannot be blamed for their unwillingness to undertake heavy work that they fear may lead to nothing. The fact that the irrigation authority has constant demands upon its services from other areas in the province where efforts are being made to introduce wet-rice cultivation or to intensify existing cultivation methods under the *Bimas* programme means that there are often delays in the construction of technical-irrigation facilities.

As is the case in most transmigration proj-ects, there is need for more attention to agri-cultural extension work. Very little thought has been given to the most suitable cropping patterns for the land cultivated by migrants, the assumption being that rice will be the major crop. It is intended that settlers should grow certain commercial crops to supplement their incomes. With the present demand local-ly and abroad for copra and the establishment since 1971 of several new processing factories in Sulawesi, the cultivation of coconut-palm would seem to be advisable, particularly since Sulawesi is climatically suited to this palm. Oil-palm could also be grown, but the need for processing facilities in the immediate vicinity would make its introduction too ex-pensive for transmigration projects at this present stage of development.

As yet, little attention has been given to the use of fertilizers; migrants have found that soil fertility is adequate for two or three years, after which there is a definite decline in yields.[15] Crop rotation could help, as could the use of animal manure. The Luwu area has an unusual advantage in the fact that there are already large numbers of cattle in the shire.[16] The cattle, however, present a problem similar to that in Bengkulu, where there are large numbers of 'wild' water-buffaloes. In both provinces the animals graze freely, doing much damage to the unfenced fields of the migrants. A further problem lies in the num-ber of insect pests that attack crops. When land has been cleared of its original vegetation and brought under cultivation, various kinds of insects invade the fields from nearby, un-cleared land. Pest control has proved to be a similar problem wherever projects have been established on land never before cultivated, though it has also been found that the prob-lem diminishes of its own accord as time passes.

The Luwu area offers possibilities for ani-mal husbandry that exist in no other settle-ment region. Plans prepared for the develop-ment of dry-farming projects during the Sec-ond Five-Year Plan involve the introduction of mixed farming, in which the raising of live-stock will provide an additional source of in-come for the migrant family. This means that animals will have to be transported to the project areas, for there is a relative shortage of livestock in the islands other than Java and the Lesser Sunda group. The Shire of Luwu, however, is a notable exception in that large numbers of cattle are already in the area. The Directorate-General for Transmigration has endeavoured to encourage the raising of cattle and, among Balinese migrants, of pigs. Settlers from East Java are pleased to have the opportunity to obtain draught animals at prices far lower than those in Java. The local people of Luwu have never attempted to use cattle in their limited farming activities. Once again, however, marketing difficulties discour-age any real expansion in animal husbandry. So far, virtually no processing or preserving of products has been attempted. Methods of pre-serving meat with various spices, so common in East and Central Java, are unknown, though as more migrants are settled in the shire these traditional skills, along with the making of soya sauce and soya bean cake, are beginning to appear.

Co-operatives have been established in five of the earlier villages in the Bone-Bone District, but they will be successful only if they can help migrants to earn additional cash income by selling products, both processed and non-processed, outside the project areas. At the present time, farmers sell whatever surplus they have to middlemen and brokers who come into settlement areas and purchase small quantities of products direct from farmers. The transmigration authority has tried to discourage this, since prices paid to farmers are very low.[17] But as long as the existing co-operatives do not have the capital, the managerial skills or the transport facilities to replace the middlemen, the practice will continue, as it does in many other parts of Indonesia.

In the actual implementation of settlement work in Luwu, much has obviously been learned from past mistakes. For example, more than a thousand of the families settled in the Bone-Bone District have already been given land certificates. Although these are not land-ownership titles, it at least means that the confusion over land that has arisen in the past in places like Way Seputih can be avoided. The issuing of land certificates in the Luwu settlements has been greatly facilitated by the fact that there have been no claims to the land by local people. This emphasizes again the importance of the transmigration authority using only land already classed as state land and hence free from claims.

At the same time an effort has been made in the Luwu settlements, as in the Way Abung and Panaragan projects in North Lampung, to lay the basis for eventual transfer to the local administrative structure. Villages and hamlets have been organized in conformity with the existing system of Districts and Sub-districts that has been drawn up by the Department of Home Affairs. Each village unit is to consist of approximately 500 families, and will have the administrative officials found in ordinary villages. The Luwu transmigration villages have from the beginning been provided with health and educational facilities by the transmigration agency, which, in the case of schools, has to pay most of the teachers.

Transmigration in the Shire of Luwu is very much a part of local area development, for the manpower needed to develop the agricultural potential of the shire is lacking. Wet-rice cultivation has not been a tradition in this part of Sulawesi, where sago-flour, obtained from palms growing wild in the swamps along the coast of the Luwu plain, has provided the staple food. Only in a few places has the cultivation of dry rice been common. The local shire government is seeking to encourage local indigenous people living in the mountainous part of the shire, where they obtain a living from timber-cutting and rattan-gathering, to settle on the lowlands so that existing forest resources may be safeguarded and erosion prevented in the upper reaches of the rivers. It is hoped that greater numbers of these people will move into transmigration project areas and become sedentary farmers, learning farming skills from their fellow villagers of Balinese or Javanese origin. It has already been found that local people are eager to use project facilities, in particular educational facilities, for their children. Assimilation in the Luwu area has proved to be relatively easy, as can be seen from the way in which the Javanese settlers placed near Bone-Bone, Masamba, Kalaena and Lamasi in 1938–40 have fitted into local conditions, adapting their own customs in matters like housing to local patterns where of practical benefit but retaining their traditions of sedentary agriculture. This is one of the very few areas where Dutch colonization settlements did not become Javanese enclaves.

The attention given to the Luwu area since 1969 will be continued during the 1974–9 period, for it is felt that the area offers great potential for transmigration settlements.[18] Other organizations, notably the Armed Forces and the Department of Social Welfare, have also established projects in Luwu, though it is intended that during the Second

Five-Year Plan any such projects will be integrated into ordinary transmigration plans. The three Social Welfare villages for natural disaster victims, in the Mangkutana District, are now part of the Mangkutana project.

Once communications within the Shire of Luwu are improved, transmigration projects in the area should progress more rapidly. The expansion of nickel-mining at Soroako near Malili at the eastern end of the shire in the late 1970s will mean a large market for agricultural products, for basic foodstuffs will be needed regularly for the labourers to be brought over from Java. It would be a mistake, however, for settlements to depend too much upon the provision of irrigation for their future growth, since possibilities for the cultivation of non-irrigated crops and for animal husbandry could be developed. Improvement of road communications with Malili and other parts of the province will bring greater prosperity to the whole area and to the transmigration projects, including Dutch-established settlements, which have tended to stagnate after reaching a certain level of self-sufficiency because of inadequate outlet for products.

During the Second Five-Year Plan, more migrants will be sent to the Luwu area. Projects will also be established in the Shire of Mamuju on the north-western coast of South Sulawesi. This part of the province is even more sparsely populated than Luwu; lack of communications makes it even more isolated from the main centres of economic activity in South Sulawesi, so a large input in the form of basic infrastructure will be necessary if projects are to prosper.

The Province of South Sulawesi every year loses quite a number of its people to other parts of the archipelago for many, particularly from the southern parts of the province, are by tradition sailors and merchants. Many, too, are attracted by the prospects offered by timber-felling companies in East Kalimantan. Irrespective of the accuracy of the report that around ten thousand people left the province in a four-month period at the end of 1973 and early 1974,[19] it appears that there is very little outward flow from the Shire of Luwu and that an inward flow of unsponsored migrants from Java and Bali is starting to develop, as has happened in other provinces of Sulawesi. There is every expectation that the Luwu area will expand into a firmly based agricultural production area.

The Province of Central Sulawesi

Central Sulawesi is perhaps the least developed section of the island, for it consists largely of very mountainous land with an extremely narrow coastal plain. Road networks are limited and the only effective means of communication with other parts of the island is by boat. Several transmigration projects were established during the 1960s but development has been slow because projects were scattered throughout the entire province at long distances from each other and from the main communication routes. In 1974, six of the pre-1969 projects, containing a total of 6 827 people, had not yet been transferred to the local provincial government.

Not all of the projects in Central Sulawesi have failed to develop, however. Those located close enough to the coast to make possible the sale of products have done well; the Parigi settlements in the Shire of Donggala have prospered to the point where it was possible to introduce the *Bimas* intensification programme on 168 hectares of rice-land in the 1972–3 planting season.[20] One significant fact in the Central Sulawesi projects has been the large number of independent migrants, in most instances Balinese, who have moved to the area entirely at their own expense or with only limited help (mainly in transportation) from the transmigration agency. They have settled for the most part in the Parigi area, where there are now twelve villages of migrants. Of the 15 074 migrants who settled in the province between 1969 and 1974, 8 539 (all of them from Bali) went to Parigi. Wherever they settle, the Balinese have proved to be excellent migrants, and their superior skill in the cultivation of irrigated rice on terraced fields has been a great asset to the settlement area.

During the First Five-Year Plan, only two new projects were opened in Central Sulawesi. In view of communication problems, the policy has been adopted of encouraging expansion in the older coastal settlements by placing more independent migrants in them. In addition to those who went to Parigi, unsponsored migrants were also sent to Rowa (707 people) and Toili (1 400 people) in the Shire of Luwuk Banggai. Much of northern Sulawesi suffers from a shortage of rice, since local people tend to be smallholders producing copra. Migrants in coastal settlements like Parigi have no trouble in selling all the rice they can produce, for rice-merchants travel by boat from places around the Gulf of Tomini to purchase rice directly from the transmigration settlements at harvest time.[21]

Of the two new projects opened for fully sponsored migrants, one is in the interior of the island near Kamba on the Lembontonara Tableland, in the Shire of Poso; 2 409 migrants were settled there in 1972–3. The project area of 3 500 hectares was made available by the provincial government, which is keen to have more of the interior of the province developed. The new project has had the advantage of no land disputes, for it is state land and virtually unpopulated. Also it is unforested, which has made it relatively easy for migrants to bring the land under cultivation after removing the original vegetation of low scrub and grass.[22] It does, however, have the disadvantage of being in a remote area; road communications with Poso, 112 km away, are very poor, which means that marketing of products will be difficult. This will be overcome when the Trans-Sulawesi Highway is completed, for the road will pass through the Poso Valley. A local road, linking the project area to the highway, will make it possible for settlers to make use of harbour and marketing facilities in the town of Poso and also to com-

municate with projects established on the Luwu plain on the southern side of the mountains that form the border of the province.

A second new project was opened at Mepanga on the northern peninsula of Sulawesi, not far from the border between Central and North Sulawesi, and 2 019 migrants were settled there in 1973–4. With the concentration of larger numbers of people in each settlement, it is hoped that economic growth will be more rapid than it has been in past years.

The Province of South-east Sulawesi

This province, like Central Sulawesi, also suffers from problems of communication, though in the case of the south-east peninsula, the terrain is less mountainous and the broad valley formed by the Koneweha and its tributaries makes road-construction far easier. This lowland area, however, has the problem of fairly extensive stretches of badly drained land, in some parts covered by swamps. This part of Sulawesi was considered for transmigration purposes only in the late 1960s, when a project was established at Amoito in 1968, for the placement of 1 396 migrants. During the First Five-Year Plan, more projects were opened and 9 011 migrants were settled in the province.

Economic growth in the Province of South-east Sulawesi has been slow and transmigration is looked upon by the provincial government as a major means of encouraging land development and of bringing new agricultural techniques to the local people.[23] An attempt has been made to resettle numbers of local people in transmigration villages in the hope of obtaining better utilization of land. The local people of the province obtain a livelihood from shifting cultivation, though with the demand in Java and abroad for timber and rattan, many have left their fields permanently to gather forest products.

The projects established have all been located fairly close to the Kendari-Kolaka road, which is the only road of any significance in the province. It links the provincial capital of

Kendari on the eastern side of the peninsula with the town of Kolaka (close to the state-owned nickel-mines) on the western side. On the whole the projects are doing well, though they suffer from the effects of the very long dry season. With only non-technical irrigation, they have no way of ensuring a supply of water for the dry season.[24] Added to this is the fact that soils are not very fertile. If any development is to take place in this province, a further input of manpower is essential, along with the knowledge of sedentary agriculture that migrants from Bali and Java possess. With existing conditions in the province, there is virtually nothing to attract manpower to the area. Most of the migrants already settled in the area have been fully sponsored, while some have been placed there under sectoral programmes prepared by the local provincial government and the governments of provinces in Java. Natural disaster victims have also been settled in the area. Relatively few independent migrants have as yet moved into the province, and much remains to be done before there will be a sufficiently strong pull-factor to draw migrants to this area when more attractive areas are available in the Luwu and the Parigi districts.

The Province of North Sulawesi

One of the first four projects established by the Indonesian transmigration authority after independence was the settlement made at Paguyaman in North Sulawesi in 1953. Since it progressed well, migrants were sent· there throughout the 1950s. When finally transferred to the provincial government in 1968, the project had well over 4 000 settlers.

In 1963 a project was established in the Dumoga area. The main purpose was to accommodate some of the victims of the Mt. Agung eruption in Bali. Two villages were established, Werdhi Agung (1963) and Kembang Mertha (1964). Despite limited assistance from the transmigration authority, both villages have prospered, for the Balinese here have proved as industrious and as resourceful

as they have in other transmigration projects. The location was well chosen, since local terrain made Balinese-style irrigation possible, soil was fertile and no disputes occurred with local people about land matters. The population of the two villages had risen from the original 2 437 settlers to a total of 3 194 in 1972 as a consequence of births and of the arrival of independent migrants attracted to the district from Bali. A total area of 1 270 hectares is under cultivation, the major crops being rice, corn, soya beans and coconuts, all of which can be marketed easily. All the original settlers in the two Dumoga villages have been given land-ownership certificates for 2 hectares of land per family.[25]

The provincial government of North Sulawesi, faced with the need to import 100 000 tonnes of rice annually, is endeavouring to extend rice cultivation in the Paguyaman (Shire of Gorontalo) and the Dumoga (Shire of Bolaang Mongondow) districts.[26] In the former area, about 15 000 hectares can be irrigated, while in the latter, 21 000 hectares can be brought under cultivation if water and cultivators are available. World Bank assistance has been provided to help with the construction of fully technical irrigation facilities in both areas and with the building of a highway from the provincial capital at Manado to the western end of the province. The road will pass through the Dumoga transmigration settlements and ultimately through the Paguyaman settlements also. All new transmigration projects will therefore be concentrated in the vicinity of the two older projects.

In 1971 a new project was established at Tumokang in the Dumoga district and sixty families were settled there. This has proved to be another instance of conflict between transmigration plans and plans formulated by other departments. The provincial government had originally given this stretch of land to the transmigration authority for settlement purposes, since the soil is fertile and the land well watered. But with the preparation of plans for the Duloduo Dumoga Dam, which will be part of the irrigation network mentioned above, the whole area has to be left under forest cover and the present site of the village of Tumokang will ultimately be under water when the dam is completed.[27] Hence the transmigration authority has been obliged to resettle the 299 people of the village in a new project first opened in September 1972 on 3 000 hectares of land at Tapadaka (Mopuya) in the Dumoga Kiri district. This new settlement has been designed on the tri-partial system in which one-third of the land is used for fully sponsored migrants, one-third for independent migrants and the resettlement of local people, and the remaining third for the future expansion of commercial-crop cultivation. In the 1972–4 period, 2 495 fully sponsored migrants were settled at Tapadaka, along with the 299 settlers from Tumokang, while 724 people were placed in an extension of the much older Paguyaman project.

With a population density of 71 persons to the sq km in 1971, North Sulawesi does not need new settlers as urgently as do the other provinces of the island, and hence it has not been included among the eleven priority provinces for transmigration during the Second Five-Year Development Plan.

The Eastern Provinces

In the more easterly parts of Indonesia, very little attention has been given to transmigration possibilities, largely because of the distance from Java and Bali and the comparative lack of infrastructure needed for economic development. Despite this, one of the first projects established after independence was that at Kairatu on the island of Seram in the Province of Maluku. In 1954, 414 migrants were settled there, followed by another 433 people in 1955; after that no further settlement was made until 1971, when a second project was opened in the Kairatu area. Migrants were sent there in 1971, 1972 and 1973, bringing the total number in the new project to 1,713.

Land problems have impeded the progress of the older settlement, since there have been no clear distinctions between state land and land held by local people under communal tenure. Added to this is the fact that the forestry authority has set aside certain areas for wild-life sanctuaries. Even more of an obstacle has been the problem of marketing. Irrigation is available in the project but it is hard for migrants to sell their excess products, although there is a constant demand for rice in Ambon. The distance is not great but lack of ships large enough to face the extremely heavy waves common in this region makes it almost impossible for farmers to transport their products to Ambon, which is virtually the only market centre.

In 1966, plans had been made for the settlement of 700 families in the District of Kao on the northern peninsula of the island of Halmahera, also in the province of Maluku.[28] However, they were not carried out even though preparatory measuring of land and construction of barracks had been done. In 1972 another survey was made of the same region but, despite the fact that land was available and traditional law did not exist in the area, it was decided not to go ahead with plans for a project, for any migrants settled in Halmahera would face the same problems of marketing as farmers in the Kairatu projects, which are far closer to potential markets than is Kao.

Although it is intended that approximately 200 families will be moved to Maluku each year during the Second Five-Year Plan, actual implementation presents great difficulties. New settlements will have to be in the immediate vicinity of the two Kairatu projects, since all facilities and equipment owned by the transmigration authority are concentrated there. The island of Seram has very few roads, which makes the location of projects in the interior virtually impossible. Since no solution has been found to land problems, areas available for settlement must remain small and new undertakings will in fact represent a fur-

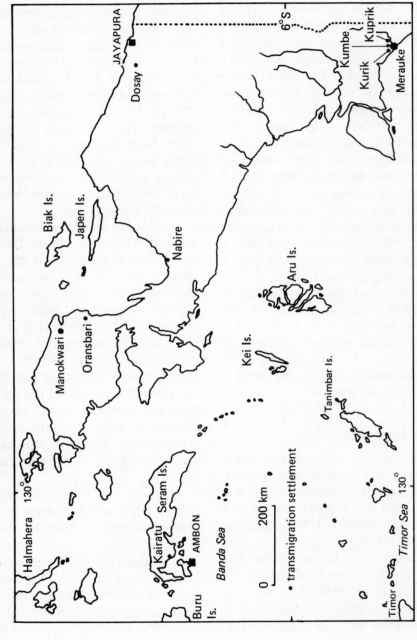

Map 8:   Maluku and Irian Jaya: transmigration settlements, 1950–1974

ther extension of the original Kairatu project.

Irian Jaya, like Maluku, has not been included in the priority provinces for transmigration during the 1974–9 period. Geographical conditions within the island, as well as distance from Java, have always discouraged the establishment of projects in Irian Jaya, while political considerations during the 1950s and early 1960s made the establishment of projects in this part of Indonesia impossible.

A few very small transmigration settlements have been attempted in Irian Jaya. The first was made in the mid-1960s, when the policies that guided the National Transmigration Movement favoured the establishment of projects in every province, irrespective of economic feasibility. In the years before 1969, five more very small settlements were made at locations scattered throughout the province. Three of these (Kumbe, Kurik and Kuprik) are grouped together as the Merauke project, for they are located in the Shire of Merauke, in the south-eastern part of the province. Of the others, one is located at Dosay, several miles inland from Jayapura, the second in the vicinity of the town of Nabire in the Shire of Paniai and the third at Oransbari, in the Shire of Manokwari. Before 1969, only 267 families were moved to these different settlements, which were so small that they could hardly be called projects. The settlement near Nabire, for example, had only eleven families. In 1971 the provincial government of Irian Jaya moved 160 families from Java to three of the existing settlements; since this was financed entirely by the provincial government, these migrants are not included in the statistics of the Directorate-General for Transmigration for that year. In 1972–3 the Directorate-General moved fifty families to Nabire and another fifty families to Oransbari, bringing the total number of people living in the six villages to 2 539. No migrants were settled in the last year (1973–4) of the First Five-Year Plan, but at the beginning of 1975, 200 families are to go to Nabire, where 15 000 hectares have been set aside for settlements.

The lack of overall development in Irian Jaya (population density only 2 persons to the sq km in 1971) has hindered the growth of the settlements, which are far too small to have any impact upon regional growth. In a province the size of South-east Sulawesi or in a relatively limited area like the Shire of Luwu, there is every possibility that transmigration can provide some of the requirements, such as manpower and agricultural skills, needed for economic growth in the region. But in the face of the natural limitations that exist in Irian Jaya, settlements would have to be on a huge scale to have any impact. This would be self-defeating in itself, for the lack of local markets means that the demand for agricultural products is limited. Large-scale projects could not operate profitably unless they were designed for the cultivation of cash crops such as oil-palm, for which there is a good market in Java and overseas. Alternatively, projects could be orientated towards logging. But the very problems of inaccessibility and transportation that discourage private entrepreneurs from taking up timber concessions in this island would also impede transmigration projects of the same kind.

In the meantime, the existing projects in Irian Jaya are faced with a problem that has not arisen anywhere else. The Javanese migrants have been encouraged to grow rice, but they cannot sell it at a profit, since the provincial government brings rice into the province at a greatly subsidized price, in an attempt to keep market prices stable.[29] The migrants cannot produce rice at a price low enough to compete with this. Rice is mainly in demand in the larger towns like Jayapura and Merauke, where other foodstuffs, like fruit and vegetables, are disproportionately expensive. Hence migrants have been giving their attention to the cultivation of crops like soya beans, groundnuts, corn and vegetables, and also to the cutting of timber for sale. If the policy of the provincial government 'to be able to be self-sufficient in rice supplies by the end of the Second Five-Year Plan'[30] is to be carried out, then clearly the existing transmigration projects will have to be extended or new ones established, so that more land can be brought under rice cultivation. Since the local people of the province have no traditions of either wet or dry rice cultivation, a large input of migrant manpower will be required, along with irrigation facilities and fertilizers, for soils in most areas have proved to be rather infertile after land has been cleared. Transmigration plans, however, allow for the settlement of only 2 500 families in Irian Jaya in the 1974–9 period.

With the present policies that are to guide transmigration during the Second Five-Year Development Plan, it seems unlikely that much attention will be given to the eastern part of Indonesia. With land still available in Sumatra, Kalimantan and Sulawesi, where attention is already being given to road construction, transmigration undertakings will continue to be concentrated on areas where economic expansion can be expected to take place in a relatively short time. Yet, as population continues to increase in Java, it is very likely that in the 1980s migrants may have to be settled in Irian Jaya, despite geographical obstacles, through lack of land elsewhere.

[1] *Kumpulan Reportase Pengawalan dan Survey Transmigrasi Tahun 1967*, op. cit., p. 19.

[2] Ibid., p. 30.

[3] *Laporan Penyelenggaraan Transmigrasi di Kalimantan Timur Dalam Pelita I*, Transmigration Directorate for East Kalimantan (Samarinda, 1974), p. 8.

[4] Ibid., p. 5.

[5] *Laporan Pelaksanaan Pelita I Proyek Transmigrasi Kalimantan Selatan*, Transmigration Directorate for South Kalimantan (Banjarmasin, 1974), Table 7.

[6] *Laporan Survey Explorasi Proyek Transmigrasi Barambai dan Jelapat Kalimantan Selatan*, Directorate-General for Transmigration (Jakarta, 1972), pp. 13, 15 and 17.

[7] Ibid., p. 5.

[8] *Projek Transmigrasi Barambai Kalimantan Selatan: Survey Pendahuluan*, Directorate-General for Transmigration (Jakarta, August 1969), p. 8.

[9] *Program, Progress & Prospek*, op. cit., p. 20.

[10] *Laporan Survey Checking Explorasi Persiapan Perluasan Penempatan Proyek Transmigrasi Tamban Luar Kalimantan Tengah*, Directorate-General for Transmigration (Jakarta, 1972), p. 8.

[11] This river, the major waterway of West Kalimantan, should not be confused with the much smaller river of the same name in Central Kalimantan.

[12] *North Luwu Plain* (a study compiled by P.N. Waskita Karya in co-operation with Investors' & Development Consultants Ltd., Jakarta), Directorate-General for Water Resources, Ministry of Public Works and Power (Jakarta, April 1970).

[13] Achmad Lamo, Governor of South Sulawesi, 'The Role of Transmigration in Regional Development in South Sulawesi' in *Transmigration in the Context of Area Development*, op. cit., p. 7.

[14] The harbours are Palopo, Wotu and Munte; Malili harbour is being improved by a nickel-mining company operating in the vicinity.

[15] *Transmigrasi di Sulawesi, 1972–1973*, Transmigration Directorate for South Sulawesi (Ujung Pandang, 1973), p. 24.

[16] According to local accounts, the cattle were introduced into the area during the Second World War, when a Japanese army base was set up at Masamba to provide food supplies.

[17] *Transmigrasi di Sulawesi, 1972–1973*, op. cit., p. 34.

[18] *Preliminary Report on the Workshop Concerning Area Development in the Bone-Bone–Mangkutana Districts of Luwu, South Sulawesi*, Directorate-General for Transmigration (Jakarta, September 1973), p. 9.

[19] *Kompas*, Editorial, 27 March 1974, p. 4.

[20] *Transmigrasi di Sulawesi 1972–1973*, op. cit., p. 29.

[21] *Program Kerja Transmigrasi di Sulawesi Tengah Tahun 1973/74*, Transmigration Directorate for Central Sulawesi (Palu, 1973), p. 3.

[22] *Laporan Survey Explorasi Calon Proyek Transmigrasi Kamba Sulawesi Tengah*, Directorate-General for Transmigration (Jakarta, 1972), p. 22.

[23] *Laporan Survey Explorasi Calon Proyek Transmigrasi Tinondo Sulawesi Tenggara*, Directorate-General for Transmigration (Jakarta, 1972), pp. 1-2, and 24.

[24] Ibid., p. 25.

[25] *Laporan Tahunan Direktorat Transmigrasi Propinsi Sulawesi Utara 1972*, Transmigration Directorate for North Sulawesi (Manado, 1972), pp. 9-10.

[26] 'Proyek Penempatan Transmigrasi di Propinsi Sulawesi Utara' in *Project Statement Program Pembangunan Transmigrasi Pelita II*, op. cit. (no page numbers).

[27] *Laporan Tahunan Direktorat Transmigrasi Propinsi Sulawesi Utara 1972*, op. cit., p. 9.

[28] *Survey Explorasi Tanah dalam Rangka Perluasan Penempatan Transmigran di Ketjamatan Kao di Pulau Halmahera*, Integrated Consultants Ltd. (Jakarta, 1972), p. 27.

[29] *Laporan Tahun 1972–73*, Transmigration Directorate for Irian Jaya (Jayapura, 1973), p. 31.

[30] Ibid., p. 32.

VII
Future Prospects

WITH the commencement of the Second Five-Year Development Plan (April 1974–March 1979), transmigration is receiving even more emphasis than it did during the First Five-Year Plan. There is increased community awareness of the significance of transmigration, largely as the result of a deepening realization of the seriousness of population problems in Java and Bali, a wider understanding of the real significance of the present deterioration of the natural environment in certain parts of Java, and a more general appreciation of the fact that regional development in the less populated parts of the country is essential in the interests of the nation as a whole. The government attitude to transmigration, as expressed in the Second Five-Year Plan, is a continuation of that in the First Plan:

In view of the number of developmental objectives that are linked with the transmigration programme, it is clear that this programme cannot be separated from developmental undertakings either during the Second Five-Year Development Plan or during the period that follows.[1]

Both the national-level government and the provincial governments are giving more attention to the incorporation of transmigration projects into plans for the development of each province and of groups of adjacent provinces that form natural regions. As has already been mentioned, three priority regions—southern Sumatra (the Provinces of Lampung, South Sumatra, Jambi and Bengkulu), West Kalimantan, together with south-eastern Kalimantan, along the road under construction between Banjarmasin, Balikpapan and Samarinda, and southern Sulawesi (the Provinces of Central, South and South-east Sulawesi)—have been selected for major transmigration undertakings during the Second Plan.[2] These regions have been chosen because they offer definite possibilities for reasonably rapid economic growth, given the advantages that will result not just from additional manpower but also from the input of facilities and infrastructure associated with transmigration projects.

Very largely as a consequence of the success attained during the last two years of the First Five-Year Plan in the field of transmigration, the targets, in terms of numbers of families to be moved during the Second Plan, have been raised considerably. It is anticipated that between 1974 and 1979, a total of 250 000 families will be moved under fully sponsored (general or *umum*) transmigration, while efforts will be made to encourage another 200 000 families to move as entirely independent migrants. This figure of 250 000 families represents a significant increase over the numerical achievements of the First Plan (1969–1974), when only 39 727 families were moved from Java, Bali and Lombok.[3] In this period 181 696 people left the three areas from which transmigration is considered to be necessary under the official programme of the Directorate-General for Transmigration; it is hoped that 1¼ million people (five persons to a family) will be moved during the Second Plan.

Although demographic considerations are by no means the basic consideration in the fixing of these targets, since it is no longer expected that transmigration can possibly keep pace with population increase in Java, it must be admitted that provincial governments in Java still tend to look to transmigration as a partial solution to some of their more urgent problems. They cannot be blamed for taking this attitude, for it is essential that large numbers of people be moved as soon as possible from the more seriously eroded parts of Java, like the Upper Solo River basin. Deforestation and the cultivation of food crops like cassava on very steep slopes give rise to rapid erosion, which affects not only the immediate vicinity but also areas further downstream, where floods are becoming a greater threat every year. The essential aim, as far as provincial governments in Java are concerned, is to have a certain number of people leave the more critical areas, so that measures can be taken to ensure that the erosion process is halted. The emphasis is on Central and East Java, from each of which approximately 100 000 families are to be moved, since these parts of Java are suffering more from the effects of erosion than is West Java. Within these provinces, priority is to be given to districts where population density is over 1 000 persons per sq km, where natural disasters like floods and volcanic eruptions threaten constantly, and where land is in such a critical condition that rehabilitation must be undertaken immediately.[4] Added to this is the fact that the Department of Public Works is planning the construction of more high-level dams in Java during the Second Development Plan, in an attempt to reduce floods during the wet season and to make more water available for irrigation during the dry season; it has already been pointed out to the transmigration authority that those people living in areas to be inundated will have to be moved within the next five years.

At the other end of the transmigration story, provincial governors outside Java have become more enthusiastic about the advantages that the establishment of transmigration projects can bring to their respective provinces. While reasons for their enthusiasm may certainly vary, depending upon the present level of economic development and the nature of existing resources in the provinces concerned, it is a good sign that the apathy once characteristic of most provincial governments outside Java, as far as the actual implementation of transmigration was concerned, has disappeared.[5] The interest shown by various international agencies in transmigration in recent years has helped to strengthen the confidence of provincial governments in the entire programme. The president of the International Bank for Reconstruction and Development, for example, was quoted as saying, after a visit to the Lampung projects, that: 'World Bank aid to Indonesia will be continued, and priority will be given to population, transmigration and agricultural projects, especially those for peasants and smallholders.'[6]

The government's objectives in transmigration have been stated clearly in the Second Five-Year Development Plan. To attain these objectives certain basic policies have been established.

The fundamental aim in transmigration is to encourage an ever-increasing flow of completely independent migrants who move with no assistance from overpopulated areas to places where employment opportunities are better. This, it is true, has always been a basic concept, but prior to the First Five-Year Plan no serious thought was given to ways of establishing a spontaneous movement of migrants. If regional development outside Java reaches a point where job opportunities prove attractive, more people will automatically be encouraged to move. Thus if transmigration projects become centres of economic growth, migrants seeking work in all fields, not just in agriculture, will be drawn to them. At the same time it is also realized that, if real effects of a positive nature are to be felt in the economies of the receiving areas, there must be large-scale migration. Present policy is directed towards this and hence targets are high, though policy-makers are very conscious of the failures of the 1950s and early 1960s, when impossibly high targets were set. In all cases the number of people to be moved is to be in accordance with the amount of land already prepared for settlement and the facilities already made available; in other words, people will not be moved to sites where preparations have not been completed, merely for the sake of reaching targets.

Government-sponsored transmigration is attempting to concentrate on the establishment of 'growth centres', that is, projects which can develop into relatively prosperous areas within a fairly short period and which will be able to attract completely independent settlers. This has in fact happened in Belitang in South Sumatra and Parigi in Central Sulawesi, as well as in the older colonization area around Metro in Lampung. While it must be admitted that geographical conditions helped to make these areas comparatively progressive and hence attractive to unsponsored migrants, it is by no means impossible to establish similar settlements even where natural conditions are less attractive, given certain elements that will lead to economic expansion.

It is obvious that there must be a fairly large input of both settlers and facilities, to avoid failures due to insufficient numbers of people or inadequate infrastructure. The plan now is to have at least ten village units, of approximately 500 families each, concentrated in one area. Ultimately one of these villages should grow into a small township, capable of providing services for the immediate farming area. With more people settled in the same vicinity, economies of scale will be possible in work such as land clearing, road construction and the provision of processing and transport facilities for agricultural products. If 5 000 families are to be settled fairly close to each other, the use of machinery for initial land clearing and later for other farm tasks becomes much more feasible than it was in the past, when groups of less than 200 families were placed in one village many kilometres from any other kind of settlement.

This policy is closely related to another policy, namely, that a settlement area should be established in such a way as to facilitate its ultimate incorporation into the existing pattern of administration in the provinces outside Java. A recent step forward, from the point of view of general provincial administration, has been the sub-division of all provinces into shires (*kabupaten*) and of all shires into districts (*kecamatan*). Thus it is no longer pos-

sible for a transmigration project or village unit to be outside the scope of administration of the local *kecamatan*. The problems that arose in the past over *marga* land no longer exist. Although the project head is responsible for the development of the project during the five-year guidance period, relations with the local government structure are established from the very beginning of the settlement. Since all village institutions such as the Village Deliberative Body and the Village Social Institute, as required by the Department of Home Affairs, are likewise established from the first years of settlement, transfer to the local administration will present no problems.[7] At the same time integration between local people and newcomers is encouraged from the beginning, for with this new administrative policy no land of an 'enclave' nature is to be left within project areas. It should be pointed out that the participation of the local government is in no way intended to reduce the authority of the transmigration agency in project development during the five-year pre-transfer period, or its responsibility for village economic growth during that time.

The establishment of larger settlements will have more impact on the development of the local area. The local economy will benefit significantly from the opening up of new land and the presence of additional manpower as greater quantities of agricultural products begin to pass through local markets. The facilities that can feasibly accompany larger projects, such as factories for processing rubber and copra, can also help the local farmer, who is at a disadvantage because of lack of processing equipment. In the last years of the First Five-Year Plan, a conscious effort was made to place new transmigration projects in the vicinity of investment areas, such as the expanding nickel-mining venture at Malili in South Sulawesi and the logging concessions in East Kalimantan. The intention is that the development of the area will be encouraged, for the agriculture-oriented transmigration projects will be able to provide foodstuffs required in non-farming undertakings.

If larger projects are to be established, then larger tracts of land, free from any claims, must be available to the transmigration agency. With the special emphasis placed upon transmigration in both the First and the Second Five-Year Plans, it has been proving easier to obtain suitable land and to settle land disputes where they have arisen, although in a few instances there have been problems over land either set aside for reserved forests or else allocated as timber concessions to private companies. The Presidential Decision stating that the land within a zone 15 kilometres wide on either side of the Trans-Sumatra Highway between Lubuklinggau in South Sumatra and Sijunjung in West Sumatra should be set aside for transmigration settlements is a most judicious one, since this section of the road passes through land that is at present sparsely populated. Improved ferry crossings between Java and Lampung, as described in the Second Five-Year Plan,[8] will help in the movement of migrants to the areas being opened up by the construction of this highway.

This leads to another policy, that of the type of land use patterns to be introduced in project areas. As a consequence of failures in past years, when irrigation was not provided in many of the projects planned on a concept of wet-rice cultivation, the policy now is to establish dry farming from the first year. It is clear that the pattern of land use predominating in Java and Bali is not necessarily the most suitable pattern for agricultural development in the other islands of the archipelago. A further consideration is the fact that, even if irrigation was regarded as essential, the Department of Public Works could not possibly provide irrigation for enough land to accommodate the large numbers of migrants to be moved between 1974 and 1979. This Department has many other demands on its services and its staff, for attention has to be given to the maintenance and rehabilitation of existing irrigation facilities in Java and Bali and in other areas where wet rice is already being grown.

More significant, however, is the fact that the transmigration authority itself is now convinced that non-irrigated farming can provide a sound basis for economic growth in settlements, as was pointed out towards the end of the First Five-Year Plan:

> For the second Pelita a new orientation will be given to the agricultural development pattern of transmigration projects, based on dry-land farming systems. . . . The introduction of mixed farming, of perennial crops in a smallholder estate pattern, the implementation of new crop rotation systems and new cultivation techniques for the improvement of marginal land conditions . . . are in one sense a problem in the economic analysis of scarce resources. . . .[9]

In the past, in projects where cash crops were not cultivated, migrants found it almost impossible to rise above the subsistence level. Even in the comparatively prosperous settlements in the Sekampung/Metro area, for example, farmers do not have much surplus rice to sell, nor do they have the land for cash-crop cultivation; hence incomes have remained low. For a time settlers in Lampung were selling large quantities of cassava, which until 1973 brought a good price. But when local prices dropped drastically as the result of a government prohibition on the export of cassava, in an attempt to divert foodstuffs to Java, migrants suffered immediately.[10] The new dry-farming policy involves the cultivation of smallholder crops like rubber. Although world market prices are not encouraging, rubber could, with good processing, bring a reasonable income to new settlers, just as it does to a large percentage of the local people of southern Sumatra and West Kalimantan. Oil-palm and coconut-palm offer even better prospects, for there is a large domestic demand as well as a good world market.

Possibilities of joint undertakings with the Directorate-General for Estates (Department of Agriculture) have also been investigated. It is hoped that migrants can be settled as smallholders on land adjacent to proposed large-scale estates to be established in southern Sumatra. The estate would provide not just processing facilities but also extension services and marketing facilities, as well as general management. The migrants, however, would be independent smallholders. The extent to which this will be possible remains to be seen, for in actual practice it may not prove to be a viable economic undertaking. Meanwhile, it is a policy worth noting in that it reflects the current concept of transforming subsistence farmers into cultivators of cash crops.

If the cultivation of cash crops is to be encouraged, 2 hectares of land per migrant family is clearly not enough, although it is an improvement upon the one hectare allocated to settlers in the colonization period. Writing of conditions in colonization settlements, Pelzer had said:

> Would it not be preferable to give the Javanese more land so that, in addition to rice and other food crops, he might grow a number of cash crops such as tobacco, coffee, pepper, and rubber, even if this meant that fewer Javanese could be settled in the Outer Islands?[11]

The transmigration authority has altered its former policy and is now allowing 5 hectares per farm family, if irrigation is not available. The Second Five-Year Development Plan states that: 'A minimum of 4-5 hectares of land is to be provided for each head of a family in cases where farming is to be done without irrigation and 2 hectares where there is irrigation.'[12] This does not necessarily mean that each family will receive full ownership rights to 4 or 5 hectares; however, it makes land available within the project area for further agricultural expansion. In the projects established since 1972–3, the present policy of a 'tri-partial' system of land allocation has been tried out.[13] The intention is that one-third of the land will be used for the immediate settlement of migrants, who will receive ownership rights to at least 2 hectares per family; one-third of the land is to be kept for

the cultivation of cash crops and for animal grazing, and one-third is to be set aside for future expansion as independent migrants move into the area, local people are resettled in the project and the children of migrants reach adulthood.

The keeping of reserve land in project areas is related to a further policy, that of introducing animal husbandry into settlements and thus establishing a pattern of mixed farming. Most farmers from Java and Bali are familiar with livestock of some kind, and virtually all are in the habit of keeping chickens or ducks. Cattle are used in East Java, particularly in Madura, and also in much of Central Java for draught purposes; goats are to be found in the drier parts of Java, with sheep in the western part of the island, where water-buffaloes predominate as draught animals. Pig-raising is common throughout most of Bali. The introduction of livestock can make available a certain amount of natural fertilizer, which is of benefit where soils are poor, while products in the form of dried meat, leather and the like can be sold readily, if there is a means of transport to market centres.

This new policy does not imply that irrigated rice projects will no longer be established. Attention will still be given to tidal projects, where rice is the major crop. This policy is the consequence of two basic lines of thought. First, Indonesia requires constantly increasing supplies of rice. Ironically, many of the provinces in the larger islands, despite their land resources, have to import rice from Java or from abroad, since local people tend to be smallholders cultivating commercial crops. Hence provincial governments like that of South Sumatra,[14] welcome tidal projects, since the increased production of rice is a direct help to the province. Second, from the point of view of availability of land, there is a tendency on the part of the government to feel that the vast expanses of swamp land in Sumatra and Kalimantan should be utilized in some manner. Special attention is to be given to the establishment of tidal projects in Jambi and later in Riau; the fact that much more pre-settlement preparation, in the form of construction of water-supply and drainage channels, must be undertaken explains why, during 1974–5, migrants will not be sent to tidal areas, though it is intended that in the second and later years of the Second Five-Year Plan large numbers of people will be settled on some of the 1 000 000 hectares of tidal land allocated for the transmigration programme.

Proposals have been made at various times for the establishment of so-called 'rice estates', using migrants as workers. The concept is that mechanization could be introduced and rice produced in very large quantities on privately owned estates. However, no satisfactory plan for implementation has ever been drawn up, largely because to expect Javanese subsistence farmers to adapt themselves to 'estate' conditions would present insurmountable problems, since rice growing of any type is in Indonesia essentially a 'small-farmer' undertaking. Furthermore, the Indonesian government is very much committed to the concept of developing smallholder agriculture and encouraging private ownership of smallholdings. This was well illustrated when suggestions made in 1973 to make use of the Way Seputih transmigration area for a 'rice estate' were rejected immediately.[15]

More attention is now being given to the cropping patterns followed both in new settlements and in those still under the care of the Directorate-General for Transmigration. A suitable rotation of crops can help maintain soil fertility. In the past, given no assistance in obtaining fertilizers and no guidance in crop rotation, migrants could do nothing but leave their holdings after eight or nine years, when fertility was exhausted by continuous cultivation of cassava. In fact they were following the traditional pattern of shifting cultivators, the difference being that land could not be made available for them to move to and hence they stayed on their holdings much longer than shifting cultivators do in either Sumatra or Kalimantan. For the migrant, the only solution has been to move to cities like Tanjungkarang and Samarinda, to work on timber concessions, or to return to Java. No real assessment has ever been made of the reasons why people have left settlements; too often it has simply been concluded that 'the people were lazy' or that 'they were not really farmers'.

However, more than just awareness of the problem of suitable cropping patterns is necessary. More extension work is required, for farmers from Java and Bali need guidance in such matters. Perhaps the most common complaint among migrant farmers, even in the more successful projects, is about the shortage of fertilizers. Many farmers who are doing moderately well feel that they could do much better if they could obtain fertilizers at a reasonable price. Of course, this complaint is by no means limited to transmigration projects. Yields in most farming areas could be increased with a greater application of fertilizer. At the same time, insecticides, even less frequently available, are needed. As pointed out in an earlier chapter, in new projects where land has to be cleared of trees and undergrowth, migrants almost always find that their crops in the first few years are troubled by insect pests whose natural habitat has been removed.

A change has also been introduced in the policy concerning fully sponsored (*umum* or general) migrants and partly sponsored (*spontan*) migrants.[16] In the past it was felt that the latter did not need the same allowances and facilities that fully sponsored migrants received. They had the initiative to move at their own expense and indeed this has always proved to be valuable 'capital'. Transmigration, however, cannot be restricted to the more enterprising members of the village community, since people have to be shifted from critical areas where employment opportunities are limited, even if they are lacking in initiative. Yet it is quite true that partly sponsored migrants have tended to make more rapid progress than fully sponsored migrants, who show an inclination to wait until things are done for them by the transmigration authority. Past experiences have indicated that if the partly sponsored migrant could receive the advantages that the fully sponsored migrant gets, in the form of land already cleared, housing, food, seed, tools and so on, these allowances, added to his initiative, would enable him to get settled more quickly. In other words, an economic 'push' should be given to those most likely to make good use of it. In any case, any classification in the settlement areas has proved to be virtually meaningless, for if crops fail due to drought, for example, all suffer equally and all need any food rations supplied by the government. Where food has been provided by the World Food Programme in Lampung and Luwu, no distinction has been made between fully sponsored or partly sponsored migrants. Therefore, all people who move in the first year of the Second Plan (1974–1975) will be classed as *umum* migrants and all will receive the same benefits. In the areas from which migrants are selected, information officers will describe only two kinds of migration, migration to ordinary farming areas and migration to tidal areas.

Another significant change in policy has occurred with the decision of the Department of Social Welfare to discontinue the establishment of separate transmigration projects for the victims of natural disasters in Java and Bali. When people ask to be moved because of floods or volcanic eruptions, the regular transmigration authority will undertake the task, though the Department of Social Welfare will continue to give on-the-spot assistance to these people. They will not be forced to migrate, but those who decide to leave their former homes will go as *umum* migrants to ordinary transmigration projects. The same applies to other groups of people, such as homeless and unemployed people from city areas, who in the past were moved to Department of Social Welfare projects. They too will be encouraged to settle as ordinary migrants outside Java.

As from April 1974, the Armed Forces have likewise decided not to establish separate projects for retired servicemen.[17] This is partly a consequence of the stipulations of the 1972 Transmigration Act, which places all authority for the implementation of transmigration in the hands of the minister concerned, and partly a consequence of the realization that all can benefit from the integration of the two transmigration programmes. Past experiences have shown that the projects established by the Armed Forces have encountered many of the same problems met with by the transmigration agency. But where transmigration projects have had to face a lack of entrepreneurship and leadership among communities of farmers still closely tied to the land, the Armed Forces projects have had an excess of these qualities and a shortage of experienced farmers. Furthermore, since the Armed Forces projects remained within the authority of the Forces concerned, there was even less integration between settlers and local people than in the ordinary transmigration settlements. Members of the Armed Forces, as they approach pension age, will be given the opportunity to become migrants and to settle in a transmigration project. The fact that many of these men have already been located outside Java and Bali during their years with the Armed Forces means that they are usually familiar with the kind of environment in which they will be placed as migrants. Those who wish to accept the opportunity—and in view of increasing unemployment in Java many have already shown interest—will be given a short course of a couple of months so that they can learn skills which will be of benefit in their new homes. Then on retirement they will be settled in projects under the Directorate-General for Transmigration. The Armed Forces will bear part of the financial burden by providing transport, housing, tools and such things for these men. The hope is that these settlers will become informal leaders in the new communities, though their status will be that of ordinary migrants, for all ties with the Armed Forces are cut when they retire. Many of them, during their years with the Forces, have acquired technical skills that will enable them to set up small repair shops for machinery and motor vehicles and to establish transport services. Usually it has been found that, in a community of farmers, very few show any interest in activities such as the organization of a truck service to transport commodities to more distant markets, where prices may be better.

The proposal is that one family out of ten in a project could be a retired serviceman and his wife and children. The age of these men will be a little higher than that of ordinary migrants, for whom the age limit is 40. The existing regulations allow for former servicemen up to 45. One problem has already arisen in the Armed Forces projects with the children of such men, for these children are usually older than those of ordinary migrants. Most are already teenagers when their parents become migrants, and hence they tend to want to move back to urban areas. On the whole, the family planning campaign has come too late to have any effect on the group of servicemen who will be retiring in the next five years; whereas an ordinary migrant family averages three children, the ex-servicemen families average six.

This policy is related to another, namely, that of encouraging non-farmers to migrate to newly developed areas. This is certainly not a new policy, for in the early 1960s it had been emphasized that transmigration must not be limited to farmers.[18] However, virtually nothing was done to implement this policy. The same concept has been restated in the Second Five-Year Plan:

Although the majority of migrants will be farmers, there is also a need for non-agricultural migrants, if a transmigration area is to develop into a social and economic unit that can continue to live and expand. For that reason policy during the Second Five-Year Development Plan involves an extension of opportunities to migrate to the non-agricultural group, in keeping with the requirements of development in the area concerned.[19]

The inclusion of this concept as a stated policy is partly a reflection of the combination of manpower and transmigration in the same ministry. However, it also indicates an awareness of the fact that a certain percentage of non-farmers could help in the development of projects on the wider scale that is now planned for the 1974–9 period.

One aspect evident in transmigration at the end of the First Five-Year Plan was the growing interest among high school 'drop-outs'. From the numbers of young men in this category who register each month at the transmigration offices in the provinces of Java, it is apparent that there is a genuine interest in migrating; these young people who have not completed high school realize that the chance of getting a good job in Java is small. Young migrants of this kind, with an educational background somewhat better than that of the average farmer yet not completely out of the rural environment, could help in the general management of village units. However, experiences in projects during 1973 and 1974 indicated that quite a large number of these 'migrants' in fact left the project areas within a year or so of settlement, presumably because they found that progress was not as rapid as they had anticipated. They have been inclined to drift to urban areas like Tanjung-karang or else to return to the cities of Java. Nevertheless, as new projects begin to develop, it is expected that such young men will remain in the settlement areas, particularly if, as is now being suggested, they are obliged to meet the requirements for ordinary migrants with regard to a minimum age and marital status (over 20 and married).

A significant step forward has been taken with the formation of a Body for the Expansion of Development in Transmigration Areas (Presidential Decree No. 29, 1974), which has the basic task of: 'co-ordinating, planning, carrying out and controlling supervision of development in transmigration areas, at both the national and the regional levels.'[20] The body exists at three levels: the national level, where overall planning and formulation of basic policies are undertaken; the provincial level, where more specific details concerning the incorporation of transmigration undertakings into plans for regional and area development are worked out; and the shire level, where actual implementation is carried out and the day-to-day problems of settlement work in projects are handled. The basic aim is to ensure better co-ordination in both planning and implementation and thus prevent some of the difficulties that arose in the past when the work of other government agencies connected with transmigration was not synchronized with the plans of the transmigration agency. The fact that the body has been established by a Presidential Decree gives considerable authority to its plans and decisions. Since representatives from other government departments are included at all three levels, it should be possible to deal more directly with such aspects as educational facilities in new settlements. With the presence of a representative of the Department of Education, the burden of providing not only schools but also staff can be shifted partly to this department. In the past the transmigration authority had to provide such facilities as long as the settlement had project status. If these other departments are involved in project planning from the very beginning, they are more likely to participate actively in the provision of facilities and services.

The same applies to the participation of the Department of Health. Health services have always proved a major problem in new settlements, since they could not be provided adequately by the transmigration agency, which has an extremely limited number of medical orderlies, nurses and midwives at its disposal. Yet while a settlement remained a project, it did not qualify for regular Health Department

services and facilities, any more than it did for the special Development Budget allowances given to all villages in Indonesia. The participation of health officials should make it possible to provide better health services and to establish family planning centres, which are very much needed in all projects. If migrants continue to have large families, it will be difficult to increase individual family prosperity. In large projects like Way Abung, the provision of schooling alone for the large number of children is a major problem.

The inclusion of the Indonesian People's Bank among the agencies represented on the Body for the Expansion of Development in Transmigration Areas points to another aspect that is now receiving more attention. Efforts are being made to provide credit to farmers at the project level. Where the *Bimas* programme has already been introduced, direct credit is available to those cultivating both irrigated and dry crops, though the farmer should already be in a position to repay such loans before credit is given. A more effective way is through local co-operatives, which have the financial support of the People's Bank and also of the Co-operative Credit Guarantees Agency, formed in 1970 to assist co-operatives.

Although the Bank will participate more directly in the provision of credit, this does not mean that the formation of co-operatives will be neglected. Emphasis will be placed upon the processing and marketing functions, where farmers' co-operatives are more likely to be successful. As the Minister for Transmigration and Co-operatives, Dr. Subroto, pointed out in an address to the People's Deliberative Assembly,

In the later growth of such regions (the transmigration settlements) the co-operative is an important instrument to be utilized in the development of the village economy, both in production and in marketing, so as to prevent the products of the migrants from falling into the hands of other people, such as the brokers and middlemen who dominate the marketing process.[21]

The link between the migrant producer and the consumer must be shortened, if the farmer is to obtain a better return for his labour. This can be done by means of a co-operative. In this context the participation of young men with some secondary education and also of former servicemen who may have had some training in administration while in the Forces is important.

If settlers are to be able to borrow money either through the *Bimas* programme or through a co-operative, they must have some kind of collateral to offer. It is here that the double significance of land titles, or at least certificates indicating ultimate right to land under cultivation, becomes apparent. With the 'Joint Decision of the Ministers for Home Affairs and for Manpower, Transmigration and Co-operatives', No. 91/1973(77/KPTS/MEN/1973), which contains stipulations for 'the giving of ownership rights to land, together with a certificate, to migrants who have settled permanently', farmers will have a land certificate that can be used to obtain bank credit. At the same time, such a certificate will encourage the new settler to work hard on his land, for it guarantees him security of tenure. The implementation of this ministerial decision has already commenced in several projects. However, it has become obvious, after experiences in the Way Seputih area, that there must be certain stipulations to prevent migrants from selling their land within a period of ten or fifteen years. Similarly, the need has long been felt for regulations to prevent the fragmentation of holdings in the new settlements. As pointed out earlier, this has

already happened to a very noticeable extent in the more successful of the Dutch colonization projects in Central and South Lampung. Legislation has been prepared to deal with these two aspects (Joint Instruction No. 25 of 1974 of the Ministers for Home Affairs and Manpower, Transmigration and Co-operatives), and there is full awareness of the significance of the matter on the part of the transmigration agency and the agency for agrarian affairs.

Perhaps the most important re-orientation in transmigration policies during the First Five-Year Development Plan is reflected in the increased emphasis on the welfare of the individual migrant and his family. This has been summed up in the Second Plan:

> ... the per capita income in the transmigration area must be better than in the area of origin. ... The aim is that the migrant, when he first arrives in this area, must feel that there is an improvement in his life and that an even better future is in store for him.[22]

If there is such an improvement and if the migrant, as an individual, is aware of it, then the basis will be laid for the movement of greater numbers of completely independent migrants. Transmigration certainly will not solve the population problems of Java and Bali, nor is it aiming to do so. Family planning is essential not just in Java but elsewhere throughout the country, and a large-scale programme has already been undertaken. Transmigration can, however, make a significant contribution to development in a country fortunate in having land and water resources that are not as yet fully utilized.

[1] *Rencana Pembangunan Lima Tahun Kedua,* op. cit., II, p. 451.

[2] Minister Subroto, 'Kebijaksanaan di Bidang Kesempatan Kerja dan Transmigrasi dalam Repelita II', *Prisma*, April 1974, p. 29.

[3] People resettled from the Gunung Balak area in Lampung are included in this figure.

[4] *Rencana Pembangunan Lima Tahun Kedua,* op. cit., II, p. 455.

[5] All four Kalimantan governors, when interviewed in July 1974, expressed great interest in having more migrants settle in their respective provinces. *Sinar Harapan*, 17 and 18 July 1974.

[6] Robert McNamara quoted in *Kompas*, 20 February 1974, p. 1.

[7] The structure of village administration in transmigration projects, along with the functions of each official, is described in detail in *Petunjuk Pembina-*

an Untuk Pembangunan Unit Desa Transmigrasi, Department of Manpower, Transmigration and Co-operatives (Jakarta, 1974).

[8] *Rencana Pembangunan Lima Tahun Kedua,* op. cit., II, p. 455. Ferry services between Merak and Panjang are to be increased and a ferry service will be introduced between Merak and Bakahuni; a road will be constructed linking Bakahuni and Gayam and the road between Gayam and Panjang will be improved.

[9] Directorate-General for Transmigration, 'Some Aspects of Regional and Rural Structures Relating to Transmigration Areas in Lampung' in *Transmigration in the Context of Area Development,* op. cit., p. 89.

[10] Government assurances that exporters would receive compensation did not prevent financial losses for farmers. *Berita Buana,* 18 July 1973, p. 1.

[11] Pelzer, op. cit., p. 230.

[12] *Rencana Pembangunan Lima Tahun Kedua,* op. cit., II, p. 456.

[13] 'Address Given by the Director-General for Transmigration on the Occasion of the Opening of the Transmigration Workshop in Lampung' (November 1973) in *Transmigration in the Context of Area Development,* op. cit., p. 52.

[14] 'Proyek Penempatan Transmigrasi Propinsi Suma-tera Selatan' in *Project Statement Program Pembangunan Transmigrasi Pelita II 1974–1979,* Buku II, op. cit. (no page numbers).

[15] 'Supposing that in this area (Way Seputih) a rice-estate were established, it can be imagined that transmigrants would easily be at a disadvantage, for the problem of competition between the requirements of the rice estate and those of transmigrants would certainly occur.' *Kompas,* Editorial, 2 August 1973.

[16] The terms *umum* and *spontan* are explained in Chapter 3.

[17] *Rencana Pembangunan Lima Tahun Kedua,* op. cit., II, p. 444.

[18] *Rantjangan Dasar Undang-Undang Pembangunan Nasional-Semesta-Berentjana Delapan Tahun: 1961–1969,* op. cit., p. 2467.

[19] *Rencana Pembangunan Lima Tahun Kedua,* op. cit., II, p. 454.

[20] Chapter II, Clause 3. *Project Statement Program Pembangunan Transmigrasi Pelita II 1974–1979,* Buku I, op. cit., pp. 22-3.

[21] 'Clarification Address on the Proposed Transmigration Bill' (29 April 1972), Directorate-General for Transmigration (Jakarta, 1972), p. 12.

[22] *Rencana Pembangunan Lima Tahun Kedua,* op. cit., II, p. 453-4.

Bibliography

A. GOVERNMENT SOURCES

1. Central Bureau of Statistics

Sensus Penduduk 1961 Republik Indonesia (*The 1961 Population Census of the Republic of Indonesia*), Jakarta, 1962.

Sensus Penduduk 1971 Republik Indonesia (*The 1971 Population Census of the Republic of Indonesia*), Jakarta, 1973.

Sensus Pertanian (*Agricultural Census*), Jakarta, 1964.

Statistik Indonesia (*Statistical Pocketbook of Indonesia*), 1957 to 1970–71 (Indonesian and English), Jakarta.

2. Department of Manpower, Transmigration and Co-operatives

(*i*) *Legislation Relevant to Transmigration*

Government Regulation No. 56 of 1958 concerning the Basis for Implementation of Transmigration (revoked in 1972).

Statute No. 29 of 1960 concerning the Basis for Implementation of Transmigration (revoked in 1972).

Joint Decision of the Minister for Cottage Industries and the Minister for Transmigration, Co-operatives and Village Community Development (No. 954/1961, No. 100) concerning a Common Blueprint for the Implementation of Basic Policies.

Joint Decision of the Minister for Agriculture and the Minister for Transmigration, Co-operatives and Village Community Development (No. 62a/KMP/1961, No. 121) concerning the Formation of a Committee for Co-operation between the Department of Agriculture and the Department of Transmigration, Co-operatives and Village Community Development.

Joint Decision of the Minister for Agrarian Affairs and the Minister for Transmigration, Co-operatives and Village Community Development (No. SK 982/KA 1961, No. 113) concerning the Formation of a Committee for Co-operation between the Department of Agrarian Affairs and the Department of Transmigration, Co-operatives and Village Community Development.

Joint Decision of the Minister for Agrarian Affairs and the Minister for Transmigration, Co-operatives and Village Community Development (No. SK 404/KA 1961, No. 114) concerning a Common Blueprint for Basic Policies.

Statute No. 5 of 1965 concerning the National Transmigration Movement (revoked in 1972).

Regulation No. 3 of 1967 of the Director-General for Agrarian Affairs and Transmigration concerning Utilization of Land in Transmigration Settlements and Land Rights for Transmigrants.

Basic Transmigration Act—Statute No. 3 of 1972, and Supplement to the Statute, No. 2988 of 1972.

Government Regulation No. 42 of 1973 concerning the Implementation of Transmigration, and Supplement to the Regulation, No. 3016 of 1973.

Presidential Decree No. 1 of 1973 concerning the Definition of Java, Madura, Bali and Lombok as Areas of Origin for Transmigration.

Presidential Decrees No. 2 and No. 12 of 1973 concerning the Definition of Certain Provinces as Transmigration Settlement Areas.

Joint Decision of the Ministers for Home Affairs and for Manpower, Transmigration and Co-operatives No. 91/1973 (77/KPTS/MEN/1973) concerning Implementation of Granting of Land Ownership Rights and Certificates to Permanently Settled Migrants.

Letter of Decision of the Minister for Manpower, Transmigration and Co-operatives

No. 420/KPTS/MEN/1973 concerning the Training and Research Centre for Transmigration.

Presidential Decree No. 29 of 1974 concerning the Formation of a Body for the Expansion of Development in Transmigration Areas.

Letter of Decree No. 1081/KPTS/MEN/1974 of the Minister for Manpower, Transmigration and Co-operatives concerning the Organization, Tasks and Working Methods of the Guidance and Implementation Bodies for Transmigration Areas.

Joint Instruction No. 22 of 1974 (16/INST/MEN/74) of the Minister for Home Affairs and the Minister for Manpower, Transmigration and Co-operatives concerning Formation of Technical Teams in Preparation for the Transfer of Transmigration Projects to Provincial Governments.

Joint Instruction No. 25 of 1974 (INS. 18/MEN/74) of the Ministers for Home Affairs and for Manpower, Transmigration and Co-operatives concerning the Granting of Land Certificates and Supervision and Protection of Land Ownership among Transmigrants.

(ii) Publications by the National-Level Directorate-General for Transmigration

A Blue-Print of Policies in the Implementation of Transmigration (Indonesian and English), Jakarta, January 1972.

Arti dan Peranan Transmigrasi di Indonesia (*The Meaning and Role of Transmigration in Indonesia*), P.T. Makarti Djaya, Jakarta, 1970.

Beberapa Saran Kearah Penjelenggaraan Integrated Project Transmigrasi Dengan Pengembangan Kelapa-Sawit (*Some Recommendations for the Establishment of an Integrated Transmigration and Oil-Palm Project*), Jakarta, 1972.

Buku Petunjuk Pelaksanaan Transmigrasi (*A Guide to the Implementation of Transmigration*), Jakarta, 1974.

Clarification Address on the Proposed Transmigration Bill by the Minister for Transmi-

gration and Co-operatives (Indonesian and English), Jakarta, April 1972.

Formulations of the Working Meeting of the Department of Transmigration and Co-operatives (Indonesian and English), Jakarta, February, 1972.

Ikhtisar Proyek-Proyek Transmigrasi Luwu Sulawesi Selatan (*A Summary of Transmigration Projects in Luwu, South Sulawesi*), Jakarta, August, 1973.

Konsep Pertama Rencana Transmigrasi Pelita II Tahun 1974 s/d 1979 (*First Draft of Transmigration Plans for the Second Five-Year Development Plan 1974 to 1979*), Jakarta, April 1974.

Kumpulan Reportase Pengawalan dan Survey Transmigrasi (*A Collection of Transmigration Introductory and Survey Reports*), Jakarta, 1967.

Land and Water Resources Development Project: The Possibilities of Making Use of Land and Water Resources in the Province of South-east Sulawesi (Indonesian and English), Jakarta, 1971.

Laporan Kegiatan Pelaksanaan Pelita Tahun II, 1970–1971 (*Report on Implementation Activities in the Second Year of the Five-Year Development Plan, 1970–1971*), Jakarta, March 1971.

Laporan Kegiatan Pengerahan dan Penempatan Dalam Pelita I Tahun ke-IV, 1972–1973 (*Report on Mobilisation and Settlement Activities in the Fourth Year of the First Five-Year Development Plan, 1972–1973*), Jakarta, March 1973.

Laporan Kegiatan Pusat Latihan dan Penelitian Transmigrasi Tahun Kerja April 1974 s/d Januari 1975 (*Report on Activities of the Transmigration Training and Research Centre from April 1974 to January 1975*), Jakarta, January 1975.

Laporan Kegiatan Tahun I Pelita 1969–1970 (*Report on Activities in the First Year of the Five-Year Development Plan, 1969–1970*), Jakarta, March 1970.

Laporan Peninjauan Proyek Transmigrasi Propinsi Bengkulu Untuk Persiapan Penem-

patan Transmigrasi Tahun 1973–1974 (Report on the Survey of Transmigration Projects in the Province of Bengkulu in Preparation for the Settlement of Transmigrants in 1973–1974), Jakarta, July 1973.

Laporan Survey Checking dan Evaluasi Objek Transmigrasi Simandolak, Indragiri Hulu, Riau (Report on the Checking and Evaluation Survey of the Simandolak Transmigration Scheme, Upper Indragiri, Riau), Jakarta, March 1970.

Laporan Survey Checking Explorasi Persiapan Perluasan Penempatan Proyek Transmigrasi Tamban Luar, Kalimantan Tengah (Report on the Exploratory Checking Survey of Preparations for Settlement Extensions in the Tamban Luar Transmigration Project, Central Kalimantan), Jakarta, March 1972.

Laporan Survey Evaluasi Proyek-Proyek Transmigrasi Sei Tambangan dan Dusun Tinggi, Sawahlunto, Sumatera Barat (Report on the Evaluation Survey of the Sei Tambangan and Dusun Tinggi Transmigration Projects, Sawahlunto, West Sumatra), Jakarta, July 1972.

Laporan Survey Explorasi Calon Proyek Transmigrasi Kamba, Sulawesi Tengah (Report on the Exploratory Survey of the Prospective Transmigration Project at Kamba, Central Sulawesi), Jakarta, 1972.

Laporan Survey Explorasi Calon Proyek Transmigrasi Mepanga, Sulawesi Tengah (Report on the Exploratory Survey of the Prospective Transmigration Project at Mepanga, Central Sulawesi), Jakarta, 1973.

Laporan Survey Explorasi Calon Proyek Transmigrasi Tinondo, Sulawesi Tenggara (Report on the Exploratory Survey of the Prospective Transmigration Project at Tinondo, South-east Sulawesi), Jakarta, 1972.

Laporan Survey Explorasi Daerah Calon Proyek Transmigrasi Ladongi-Kolaka, Sulawesi Tenggara (Report on the Exploratory Survey of the Area for Prospective Transmigration Projects at Ladongi-Kolaka, South-east Sulawesi), Jakarta, 1972.

Laporan Survey Explorasi Objek Transmigrasi Kateman, Indragiri Hilir, Riau (Report on the Exploratory Survey of the Kateman Transmigration Scheme, Lower Indragiri, Riau), Jakarta, April 1970.

Laporan Survey Explorasi Proyek Transmigrasi Barambai dan Jelapat, Kalimantan Selatan (Report on the Exploratory Survey of the Barambai and Jelapat Transmigration Projects, South Kalimantan), Jakarta, May 1972.

Laporan Survey Tjalon Daerah Transmigrasi Sei Rasau, Kalimantan Barat (Report on the Survey of the Prospective Transmigration Area at Sei Rasau, West Kalimantan), Jakarta, February 1972.

Laporan Tahunan Direktorat Djenderal Transmigrasi Tahun ke-3, Pelita I, 1971/1972 (Annual Report of the Directorate-General for Transmigration, Third Year of the First Five-Year Development Plan, 1971–1972), Jakarta, May 1972.

Lokakarya Indonesia-ACARRD (FAO/UNDP) Tentang Masalah Pembangunan Wilayah dan Transmigrasi Dengan Mengutamakan Para Petani Kecil dan Buruh Tani 1973 (The 1973 Indonesia-ACARRD (FAO/UNDP) Workshop Concerning Problems of Area Development and Transmigration With Emphasis on Small Farmers and Agricultural Labourers), Jakarta, May 1974.

Miniatur Panel Direktorat Djenderal Transmigrasi dan Direktorat Djenderal Koperasi (Panel in Miniature of the Directorate-General for Transmigration and the Directorate-General for Co-operatives), Jakarta, 1972.

Penempatan Transmigran Dengan Pola Pertanian Sawah Pasang Surut di Delta Upang (Settlement of Transmigrants Following the Tidal-Irrigation Pattern of Agriculture in the Upang Delta), Jakarta, August 1974.

Perumusan Hasil-Hasil Rapat Kerdja Transmigrasi 24-27 Februari 1969 (Formulation of the Results of the Transmigration Working Meeting of 24-27 February 1969), Solo, February 1969.

Petunjuk Pembinaan Untuk Pembangunan

Unit Desa Transmigrasi (Guide-Lines for the Development of Transmigration Village Units), Jakarta, May 1974.

Petunjuk Umum Pelaksanaan Untuk Program Kerja Transmigrasi 1973/1974 Dalam Menyongsong Repelita II dan Evaluasi Pelita I (General Implementation Guide-Lines for the 1973/1974 Transmigration Work Program in Preparation for the Second Five-Year Development Plan and Evaluation of the First Plan), Jakarta, June 1973.

Pokok-Pokok Untuk Rencana Transmigrasi Repelita II dan Khususnya Rencana 1974/1975 (Bases for Transmigration Plans During the Second Five-Year Development Plan and Particularly for 1974/1975 Plans), Jakarta, April 1973.

Pola Kerdja Sama Departemen Transkopemada Dengan Departemen-Departemen Lain (Blue-print for Co-operation Between the Department of Transmigration, Co-operatives and Village Community Development and Other Departments), Jakarta, no date (approx. 1962).

Pola Pengembangan Ekonomi Daerah Transmigrasi Menudju Pembangunan Desa Baru (Blue-print for Economic Expansion of Transmigration Areas Leading to the Development of New Villages), Jakarta, December 1970.

Pola Tata Ruang Pasang Surut Tahun III Pelita 1971–1972 (Blue-print for Tidal-Project Layout, Third Year of the Five-Year Development Plan, 1971–1972), Jakarta, 1971.

Preliminary Report on the Workshop Concerning Area Development in the Bone-Bone—Mangkutana Districts of Luwu, South Sulawesi (Indonesian and English), Jakarta, September 1973.

Project Statement Program Pembangunan Transmigrasi, Pelita II, 1974–1979 (A Project Statement of the Transmigration Development Program, Second Five-Year Development Plan, 1974–1979), Volumes I and II, Jakarta, July 1974.

Projek Transmigrasi Barambai, Kalimantan Selatan: Survey Pendahuluan (Barambai Transmigration Project, South Kalimantan: A Preliminary Survey), Jakarta, August 1969.

Promotion of Transmigration Activities in the Context of Area Development (Ujung Pandang South Sulawesi Seminar, January 1975), (English), Jakarta, 1975.

Punggur Daerah Transmigrasi Dengan Pola Pertanian Sawah Beririgasi (Punggur—A Transmigration Area With an Agricultural Pattern Based on Irrigation), Jakarta, September 1974.

Realisasi Penempatan Transmigrasi Tahun ke-IV Pelita I 1972/1973 (Achievements in Settlement of Transmigrants During the Fourth Year of the First Five-Year Development Plan 1972/1973), Jakarta, 1973.

Study Kasus Pada Proyek Transmigrasi Way Abung Dengan Pola Pertanian Kering (A Case Study of the Way Abung Transmigration Project With an Agricultural Pattern Based on Dry Farming), Jakarta, September 1974.

Summary Report on Three Case Studies in Transmigration Areas with Different Agricultural Patterns (English), Jakarta, December 1974.

The Role of Transmigration in National and Regional Development—Proceedings of the 1971 Transmigration Workshop (English), Jakarta, 1974.

The Strategy of Transmigration and Co-operatives in the Context of National Strategy (Indonesian and English), Jakarta, March 1972.

Transmigrasi Dalam Repelita II Tahun 1974/1975 s/d 1978/1979 (Transmigration During the Second Five-Year Development Plan from 1974/1975 to 1978/1979), Jakarta, August 1973.

Transmigrasi, Koperasi dan Pembangunan Masjarakat Desa 1959–1962 (Transmigration, Co-operatives and Village Community Development 1959–1962), Jakarta, January 1962.

Transmigration as Related to Small and Landless Farmers in Indonesia (Country Report to ASARRD Regional Follow-Up Seminar, Bangkok), (English), Jakarta, August 1974.

Transmigration in the Context of Area Development—Proceedings of the Workshop Concerning Area Development in Luwu, South Sulawesi, and of the Workshop Concerning Field Problems of Area Development and Transmigration in Lampung, Surakarta and Jakarta (English), Jakarta, 1974.

Way Abung Transmigration Project (English), Jakarta, September 1971.

(iii) Publications by Provincial-Level Transmigration Directorates

Province of Lampung:

Kumpulan Data-Data (Collection of Data), Tanjungkarang, November 1973.

Laporan Tahunan Tahun Kerja 1972/1973 (Annual Report for the 1972/1973 Working Year), Tanjungkarang, March 1973.

Laporan Tahunan Tahun Kerja 1973/1974 (Annual Report for the 1973/1974 Working Year), Tanjungkarang, July 1974.

Pelaksanaan Penempatan Transmigrasi Pelita I di Daerah Lampung (Settlement of Transmigrants in Lampung During the First Five-Year Development Plan), Tanjungkarang, November 1973.

Proyek Transmigrasi Way Seputih I & II (The Way Seputih I & II Transmigration Projects), Tanjungkarang, November 1973.

Rencana Penyelenggaraan Transmigrasi Dalam Pelita II di Daerah Lampung (Plans for Transmigration in Lampung During the Second Five-Year Development Plan), Tanjungkarang, October 1973.

Risalah Singkat Proyek Transmigrasi Way Abung, Kabupaten Lampung Utara (A Short Description of the Way Abung Transmigration Project, Shire of North Lampung), Tanjungkarang, October 1973.

Province of South Sumatra:

Ikhtisar Keadaan Proyek-Proyek Transmigrasi Propinsi Sumatera Selatan (A Summary of Conditions in Transmigration Projects in the Province of South Sumatra), Palembang, 1973.

Laporan Tahunan 1972–1973 (Annual Report for 1972–1973), Palembang, June 1973.

Perkembangan dan Pengembangan Produksi Daerah Pasang Surut Delta Upang (Expansion and Development in Production from the Upang Delta Tidal Region), Palembang, 1974.

Province of Bengkulu:

Laporan Penyelenggaraan Program Transmigrasi Tahun 1972–1973 (Report on the Implementation of the Transmigration Program 1972–1973), Bengkulu, March 1973.

Laporan Tahunan 1974–1975 (Annual Report for 1974–1975), Bengkulu, 1975.

Province of West Sumatra:

Program Penyelenggaraan Transmigrasi Propinsi Sumatera Barat Tahun 1974–1975 (Program for the Implementation of Transmigration in West Sumatra in 1974–1975), Padang, 1974.

Province of Riau:

Laporan Evaluasi Ekonomi Tahun 1969 s/d 1972 (Economic Evaluation Report for 1969 to 1972), Pekanbaru, February 1973.

Laporan Tahun 1972/73 (1972/73 Report), Pekanbaru, June 1973.

Program Kerja Tahun 1973/74 (Work Program for 1973/74), Pekanbaru, June 1973.

Province of Jambi:

Perkembangan Proyek Transmigrasi Rantau Rasau (Expansion of the Rantau Rasau Transmigration Project), Jambi, March 1975.

Province of North Sumatra:

Laporan Tahunan 1972/73 (1972/73 Annual Report), Medan, 1973.

Province of East Kalimantan:

Laporan Kegiatan Tahun I-IV Pelita (Report on Activities During the First Four Years of the Five-Year Development Plan), Samarinda, March 1973.

Laporan Penyelenggaraan Transmigrasi di Kalimantan Timur Dalam Pelita I (*Report on the Implementation of Transmigration in East Kalimantan During the First Five-Year Development Plan*), Samarinda, March 1974.

Proyek Transmigrasi Bukit Biru Kabupaten Kutai Kalimantan Timur (*The Bukit Biru Transmigration Project, Shire of Kutai, East Kalimantan*), Samarinda, March 1974.

Proyek Transmigrasi Maluhu dan Sukarame Kabupaten Kutai Kalimantan Timur (*The Maluhu and Sukarame Transmigration Projects, Shire of Kutai, East Kalimantan*), Samarinda, March 1974.

Proyek Transmigrasi Samboja Kotamadya Samarinda Kalimantan Timur (*The Samboja Transmigration Project, Municipality of Samarinda, East Kalimantan*), Samarinda, March 1974.

Province of South Kalimantan:
A Short Report of Barambai Settlement (English), Banjarmasin, 1974.

Laporan Pelaksanaan Pelita I Proyek Transmigrasi Kalimantan Selatan (*Report on the Implementation of Transmigration Projects in South Kalimantan in the First Five-Year Development Plan*), Banjarmasin, March 1974.

Laporan Singkat (*A Short Report*), Banjarmasin, 1974.

Laporan Tahunan Periode April 1973 s/d March 1974 (*Annual Report for the Period from April 1973 to March 1974*), Banjarmasin, April 1974.

Province of South Sulawesi:
Pola-Pola Pemukiman (*Settlement*) *di Daerah Sulawesi Selatan dan Kemungkinan Mengembangkan Unit Desa Transmigrasi* (*Patterns of Settlement in South Sulawesi and Possibilities for Development of Transmigration Village Units*), Ujung Pandang, December 1974.

Program Kerja 1973/1974 (*Work Program for 1973/1974*), Ujung Pandang, April 1973.

Transmigrasi di Sulawesi 1972/1973 (*Transmigration in Sulawesi 1972/1973*), Ujung Pandang, August 1973.

Province of South-east Sulawesi:
Laporan Tahun Kerja 1972/1973 (*Report on the 1972/1973 Working Year*), Kendari, June 1973.

Province of Central Sulawesi:
Program Kerja Transmigrasi di Sulawesi Tengah Tahun 1973/1974 (*Transmigration Work Program in Central Sulawesi for 1973/1974*), Palu, May 1973.

Province of North Sulawesi:
Laporan Tahunan 1972 (*1972 Annual Report*), Manado, December 1972.

Province of Irian Jaya:
Laporan Singkat Pelaksanaan Pekerjaan Direktorat Transmigrasi Irian Jaya Tahun 1974/ 1975 (*A Brief Report on the Implementation of Work by the Irian Jaya Transmigration Directorate during 1974/1975*), Jayapura, 1975.

Laporan Tahun 1972–1973 (*Report for 1972–1973*), Jayapura, March 1973.

Province of Bali:
Laporan Pelita I Tahun ke-IV, 1972–1973 (*Report on the Fourth Year of the First Five-Year Development Plan, 1972–1973*), Denpasar, 1973.

3. Other Government Departments
Department of Information
Garis-Garis Besar Rentjana Pembangunan Lima Tahun 1956–1960 (*Broad Outlines of the Five-Year Development Plan for 1956–1960*), State Planning Bureau, Jakarta, 1956.

Rantjangan Dasar Undang-Undang Pembangunan Nasional-Semesta-Berentjana Delapan Tahun 1961–1969 (*Basic Legislation for Overall, Planned National Development in the Eight-Year Period: 1961–1969*), National Planning Board, Jakarta, 1960.

Rentjana Pembangunan Lima Tahun 1969/70–1973/74, Buku I, II & III (The Five-Year Development Plan for 1969/70–1973/74, Books I, II & III), Jakarta, December 1968.

Rencana Pembangunan Lima Tahun Kedua, 1974/75–1978/79, Buku I, II, III & IV (The Second Five-Year Development Plan, 1974/75–1978/79, Books I, II, III & IV), Jakarta, March 1974.

Department of Social Welfare

Himpunan Bahan-Bahan dan Hasil Rapat Kerja Masalah Tuna Karya, Direktorat Tuna Karya (Collection of Material and Results of the Working Meeting concerning the Problem of the Unemployed, Directorate for the Unemployed), Jakarta, March 1973.

Laporan Tahunan 1972–1973 Dinas Sosial Propinsi Lampung (Annual Report for 1972–1973 of the Social Service Office Province of Lampung), Tanjungkarang, March 1973.

Laporan Tahunan 1972–1973 Direktorat Jenderal Urusan Bencana Alam dan Dana Bantuan Sosial (Annual Report for 1972–1973 of the Directorate-General for Natural Disasters and Social-Assistance Funds), Jakarta, May 1973.

Pedoman Pelaksanaan Operasionil Penggarapan Masalah Tuna Karya (Guide to Operational Implementation in Handling the Problem of the Unemployed), Jakarta, April 1971.

Program Kerja Tahun Dinas 1973/1974 Direktorat Jenderal Urusan Bencana Alam dan Dana Bantuan Sosial (Work Program for the Official Year 1973/1974 of the Directorate-General for Natural Disasters and Social-Assistance Funds), Jakarta, April 1973.

Progress Report Dinas Sosial Propinsi Bengkulu (Progress Report of the Social Service Office Province of Bengkulu), Bengkulu, March 1972.

Department of Agriculture

Contribution to the Realization of the Transmigration Projects (English), Jakarta, May 1966.

The Trend Towards the Use of Solar Oil in Light Industries in West Java: Survey Report (English), Directorate-General for Forestry, Jakarta, March 1970.

Undang-undang Pokok Agraria No. 5, 1960 (Basic Agrarian Act No. 5 of 1960), Jakarta, September 1960.

Department of Public Works

Program, Progress & Prospek (Programs, Progress & Prospects), Directorate-General for Water Resources, Jakarta (no date).

Transmigration Placement Viewed from the Irrigation Aspect (English), Public Works Provincial Office for Lampung, Telukbetung, November 1973.

B. NON-GOVERNMENT SOURCES

Amral Sjamsu, M., *Dari Kolonisasi Ke Transmigrasi (From Colonisation to Transmigration)*, Djambatan, Jakarta, 1960.

Bambang, S., 'Lampung Masih Membutuhkan Tambahan Penduduk' ('Lampung Still Needs Additional Population'), *Kompas*, 10 February 1973.

Daldjoeni, N., 'Dua Visi Tentang Pendekatan Kulturil di Daerah Transmigrasi' ('Two Visions of Cultural Approach in Transmigration Areas'), *Kompas*, 20 January 1973.

Food and Agriculture Organization of the United Nations, *Report of the Special Committee on Agrarian Reform*, Rome, August 1971.

Fisher, C.A., *South-east Asia*, Methuen & Co., London, 1964.

Hadisapoetro, Soedarsono, 'Badan Usaha Unit Desa dan Masalah Pembinaannya' ('Village Enterprise Units and the Problem of their Development'), *Prisma*, August 1973, pp. 31-42.

Hady, Hariri, 'Pembangunan Daerah Dalam Repelita II' ('Regional Development During the Second Five-Year Development Plan'), *Prisma*, April 1974, pp. 63-70.

Hardjono, J., *Indonesia, Land and People*, P.T. Gunung Agung, Jakarta, 1971.

Hardjosudarmo, Soedigdo, `Kebidjaksanaan Transmigrasi Dalam Rangka Pembangunan Masjarakat Desa di Indonesia (Transmigration Policy in the Context of Village Community Development in Indonesia)*, Bhratara, Jakarta, 1965.

Hatta, Mohammad, 'Industri dan Transmigrasi dalam Indonesia' ('Industry and Transmigration in Indonesia') (Chapter VI, p. 69) and 'Kooperasi Dasar Transmigrasi, Bukan Foedalisme' ('The Co-operative, Not Feudalism, as the Basis of Transmigration') (Chapter VII, p. 79) in *Beberapa Fasal Ekonomi (Some Economic Concepts)* Vol. I, 4th edition, Balai Pustaka, Jakarta, 1950.

Institute of Agriculture, Bogor, *Laporan Survey ke Daerah Merauke, Irian Barat (Report on a Survey of the Merauke Area, West Irian)*, Bogor, May 1970.

Integrated Consultants Ltd., *Survey Explorasi Tanah dalam Rangka Perluasan Penempatan Transmigran di Ketjamatan Kao di Pulau Halmahera (Land Exploration Survey in the Context of Further Settlement of Transmigrants in the District of Kao on the Island of Halmahera)*, Jakarta, June 1972.

Irwaty, 'Transmigrasi dan Masalahnya di Propinsi Bengkulu' ('Problems of Transmigration in the Province of Bengkulu'), *Kompas*, 16 January 1974.

Koentjaraningrat and Bachtiar, H.W., (ed.) *Penduduk Irian Barat (The People of West Irian)*, P.T. Penerbitan Universitas, Jakarta, 1963.

Legge, J.D., *Indonesia*, Prentice-Hall Inc., New Jersey, 1964.

Mangkusuwondo, Suhadi, Joedono, S.B., and Kuntjoro Jakti, Dorodjatun (ed.), *Prospek Perekonomian Indonesia 1973 (Prospects for the Indonesian Economy in 1973)*, University of Indonesia, Jakarta, 1973.

McNicoll, G., 'Internal Migration in Indonesia: Descriptive Notes', *Indonesia* No. 5, April 1968, pp. 29-92.

Naim, Mochtar, 'Merantau dan Pengaruhnya Terhadap Pembangunan Daerah' ('Emigration and its Effect upon Regional Development') *Prisma*, June 1972, pp. 36-41.

Nitisastro, Widjojo, *Population Trends in Indonesia*, Cornell U.P., Ithaca, 1970.

Nugroho, *Indonesia, Facts and Figures*, Terbitan Pertjobaan, Jakarta, 1967.

Pelzer, K.J., *Pioneer Settlement in the Asiatic Tropics*, Institute of Pacific Relations, New York, 1945.

Robequain, C., *Malaya, Indonesia, Borneo and the Philippines* (trans. E.D. Laborde), (2nd edn.), Longmans, London, 1958.

Soebiantoro, R., *Problems Connected with Land Use and Land Reform in Indonesia*, Jakarta, 1970. *Some Notes on Agrarian Reform in Indonesia*, Jakarta, 1972. *Transmigrasi Dengan Prospek Prosperity dan Security (Transmigration and the Prospects It Offers for Prosperity and Security)*, (Indonesian and English), Jakarta, July 1971.

Soekmono, R., 'Geomorphology and the Location of Sriwijaya', *Madjalah Ilmu-Ilmu Sastra Indonesia*, April 1963, pp. 79-92. 'A Geographical Reconstruction of North-eastern Central Java and the Location of Medang', *Indonesia*, No. 4, October 1967, pp. 2-7.

Subroto, 'Kebijaksanaan di Bidang Kesempatan Kerja dan Transmigrasi Dalam Repelita II' ('Policies in the Field of Employment and Transmigration During the Second Five-Year Development Plan'), *Prisma*, April 1974, pp. 18-29.

Sutyoso, Yos, 'Land Development and the Settler: the Social Aspects of Land Development', Seminar on National Development, Kuala Lumpur, Malaysia, 1973.

Tjiptadi, Wachjuddin, 'Berantaslah Padang Lalang Dengan Menanam Singkong' ('Eradicate *Lalang* Grass by Planting Cassava'), *Kompas*, 1 September 1973.

Toruan, R., 'Luwu Daerah Transmigrasi Yang Paling Berhasil' ('Luwu, the Most Successful Transmigration Area'), *Kompas*, 15 November 1972.

Utomo, Kampto, 'Masjarakat Transmigran

Spontan Didaerah W. Sekampung (Lampung)' ('The Independent Transmigrant Community in the W. Sekampung Area of Lampung'), *Tehnik Pertanian*, July-Sept., 1958, pp. 273-441.

Utrecht, E., 'Land Reform in Indonesia', *Bulletin of Indonesian Economic Studies*, Vol. V, No. 3, November 1969, pp. 71-88.

Vlekke, B.H.M., *Nusantara*, (rev. ed.), Bruxelles and Jakarta, 1961.

Waskita Karya, P.N., *North Luwu Plain*, Jakarta, April 1970.

Index